The Breaking of Style

• • •

HOPKINS
•
HEANEY
•
GRAHAM

Helen Vendler

Harvard University Press

Cambridge, Massachusetts

London, England

1995

Library of Congress Cataloging-in-Publication Data

Vendler, Helen Hennessy.
The breaking of style: Hopkins, Heaney, Graham / Helen Vendler.
p.   cm.—(The Richard Ellmann lectures in modern literature)
ISBN 0-674-08120-X (cloth: alk. paper).
ISBN 0-674-08121-8 (pbk.: alk. paper)
1. English poetry—History and criticism. 2. Hopkins, Gerard Manley,
1844-1889—Style. 3. Heaney, Seamus—Style. 4. Graham, Jorie, 1951-   —Style. 5
English language—Style. I. Title. II. Series: Richard Ellmann lectures in
modern literature
PR504.V46   1995
821.009—dc20

95-4663
CIP

Acknowledgments

◆ ◆ ◆

This book was given as the Richard Ellmann Memorial Lectures (1994) at Emory University. I am most grateful to Professor Ronald Schuchard for his memorable hospitality on the occasion of my stay.

My editors at Harvard University Press, Margaretta Fulton and Maria Ascher, have made the creation of this book a pleasure.

I am indebted to Susan Welby for devoted assistance with manuscript preparation.

Author and publisher are grateful for permission to use the following material:

Citations from *The Poetical Works of Gerard Manley Hopkins,* ed. Norman Mackenzie (London, 1990), reprinted by permission of Oxford University Press.

Excerpts from "Settings" xix and "Settings" xxiv from *Seeing Things,* by Seamus Heaney, copyright © 1991 by Seamus Heaney; and excerpts from "Oysters," "Clearance" [5], "Field Work" [IV], "The Grauballe Man," and "Terminus" from *Selected Poems, 1966–1987,* by Seamus Heaney, copyright © 1990 by Seamus Heaney; all reprinted by permission of Farrar, Straus & Giroux, Inc., and Faber and Faber.

Contents

◆　◆　◆

Preface

◆ ◆ ◆

When I was twenty-seven, Harvard University Press, on the suggestion of my dissertation director John Kelleher, asked to see my work on Yeats's *Vision* and the plays, and a few months later I found in my mail a note from the Press with a reader's report recommending publication. When the book was published, I learned that my reader had been Richard Ellmann. I was always grateful to him for fostering me into print. Eventually, we grew to know each other, and to my admiration for his writing there was added an affection for the person. The issue of the *Yeats Annual* compiled in his honor became, in the event, a memorial issue; the essay I wrote, as if by a final benefaction from him, spurred me to begin at last the book on Yeats's poems that I have wanted to write since I was twenty-three.

When I falter under the burden of manuscripts, letters of recommendation, and endorsements of tenure, I remember that Richard Ellmann was not too busy, long ago, to read a manuscript written by a student, and to welcome it with generous warmth. Perhaps being married to the wonderfully intelligent Mary had made him more hospitable to writing by women than many men of his scholarly generation—or maybe, and more likely, he married Mary because he liked intelligent women. His self-deprecatory and ironic humor prevented his ever exhibiting pomposity, even when he was wearing his Oxford gown at New College, as he was when I saw him last. He was both good to me and good for me, as he was for countless younger writers. Many other scholars have, as he had, high professional accomplishments; but memorials seem to accrue to those who are not only distinguished but also loved. The tragedy of his last illness stands as an instance of life's arbitrary cruelty to the good and the gifted; but our memories of him, and the many memorials in his honor, together with his own capacious and definitive writings, ensure that we remember, with a regenerative sense of life's copiousness, his full spirit.

The Breaking of Style

Introduction

◆　◆　◆

It is still not understood that in lyric writing, style in its larges.
sense is best understood as a material body. When a poet puts off
an old style (to speak for a moment as though this were a delib-
erate undertaking), he or she perpetrates an act of violence, so to
speak, on the self. It is not too much to say that the old body
must be dematerialized if the poet is to assume a new one. "In
art, in a sense," John Ashbery wrote in *Reported Sightings,* "all
change has to be for the better, since it shows that the artist hasn't
yet given in to the ever-present temptation to stand still and that
his constantly menaced vitality is emitting signals" (187). The fears
and regrets attending the act of permanent stylistic change can be
understood by analogy with divorce, expatriation, and other such
painful spiritual or imaginative departures. It is hoped, of course,
that the new body—like the new spouse or the new country—will
be more satisfactory than the old, but it is a hope, not a certainty.

I have been speaking as though the invention of a new stylistic
body were a voluntary act, like filing for divorce or going willingly
to live abroad. But there is much that is wholly involuntary about
it. A new sense of life presses unbidden upon the poet, making
the old style seem unsuitable or even repellent. "Some of one's
early things," Wallace Stevens wrote, "give one the creeps" (*Let-
ters,* 667). Robert Lowell complained that pieces of his earlier
driven and violent style kept turning up like flotsam and jetsam
when he was trying to write the ironic, mild, and distanced lines

of *Life Studies*. The invention of a new phase of style, then, is often less a voluntary act than an involuntary one. One is repelled by one's present body and cannot inhabit it any longer.

To represent style, I use the word "body" (rather than the perhaps more customary image of dress) because I want to emphasize the inextricable relation of style to theme. Yeats's bravado in "A Coat" with respect to doffing his "old embroideries"—"There's more enterprise / In walking naked" (*Collected Poems*, 125)—suggests, misleadingly, that one *can*, in poetry, walk naked—and that one can easily slough off a style. Nothing could be further from the truth.

There are, of course, artists who do not exhibit dramatic breaks of style—Herbert, for instance. And there are some, like Tennyson, who attain a mature style and work deliberately within it for decades, complicating and elaborating it. Some poets pursue two very different styles at the same time (though usually in two different genres, as Wordsworth does in the *Lyrical Ballads* and *The Prelude*). But other artists perceive—sometimes even in extreme youth, as Keats did—that they cannot continue to write in the style that they have made, that they have even perfected. Keats, striking out the influence of Milton from *Hyperion*, declared, with no hyperbole intended, "Life to him would be death to me" (*Letters*, II, 212). And he wrote himself a new body in *The Fall of Hyperion*.

A dramatic change of literary body cannot be other than overdetermined. In consequence, many inferences about a poet's feelings can be made from style. Keats's declaration against Milton was in part religious, rejecting Milton's god; in part cultural, rejecting Milton's endorsement of Hebrew mythology over Greek mythology; in part linguistic, rejecting Milton's Latinity; in part gender-directed, rejecting Milton's principle of male sovereignty; in part political, rejecting Milton's monarchic and hierarchic heaven and earth. But rejection alone—whether it repudiates an adolescent style, as in Stevens; a mature but now repellent style, as in

Lowell; or a historical precursor's style, as in Keats—cannot by itself supply a positive model for a new body. The positive aspect of the breaking of style, when it appears, must, as much as the negative one, have a convergent set of creative causes. "English ought to be kept up," said Keats (*Letters*, II, 167), suggesting that if he did not positively keep it up, English might fade and die. "I had long had haunting my ear the echo of a new rhythm," Hopkins wrote to Richard Watson Dixon, explaining why the prosody of "The Wreck of the Deutschland" differed so from the metrics of his early verse (*Correspondence*, 14). "The goldener nude of a later day"—a positive, Botticellian idealization of the new creative Venus—beckoned to Stevens as he contemplated the present "paltry nude" of American culture (*Collected Poems*, 5–6). Seamus Heaney, writing *North*, found himself looking to the "thin" music of poetry written in the Irish language for a positive alternative body to the broad (and colonizing) placidities of the English pentameter. There must be, in short, espousals as well as rejections in the invention of the new stylistic body, not only when the new body is a permanent one but also when it is provisional, when it is adopted for a single volume or even for a single poem.

Not only aesthetic motives determine a change of style. Moral reasons, too—and at least as often as aesthetic ones, as we have seen in the case of Keats—can prompt a breaking of form. The author may be forced to admit, by a new blankness in his own perception of the world, that the absence of the (old) imagination had itself to be imagined, as Stevens put it in "The Plain Sense of Things" (*Collected Poems*, 502–503), compelling himself to face the blank that lies beneath the trials of device. We can see a comparable admission in Hopkins when he faces the truth that on the Last Day the aesthetic variety of the world will be obliterated—that earth's dapple will come to an end, and only moral choice will be left. Once such a moral admission is made, a new style must, if the writing is to remain authentic, be created to meet it and embody it. Impatient rejection, ardent and idealistic espousal, and pained admission are all motives for the struggle toward a new permanent body to replace the old.

Yet, as I have said, there are also less permanent changes of style—changes assumed for a moment, for the purposes of a single poem perhaps. It is such temporary changes that make us see two poems, even two written by their author on the same day, as different from each other. The Protean flexibility of the poetic body is always astonishing to me, and most acutely so when I am struck by a poet's variety of strategies from poem to poem, even when the poems are written in a single recognizable style. By a "single style" I mean the general characteristics by which we identify Donne, say, or Shelley—characteristics denoting a manner which we could specify with a generally agreed-upon string of adjectives and adverbs. Yet even within that specifiable style, one Holy Sonnet does not sound like another (even if both are, let us say, startling, abrupt, intense, syntactically dense, imagistically intellectual, and so on). Nor does Shelley's "Ode to the West Wind" sound like "The Cloud," though we find both of them "Shelleyan." The micro-levels of stylistic change which we must invoke to answer a question like "How does the first sonnet of Donne's *Corona* differ from the second?" need to be attended to quite as much as the macro-levels that differentiate Donne from Herbert; such micro-levels of change from poem to poem reflect changes of feeling, changes of aesthetic perception, or changes of moral stance in the poet.

Finally, between the macro-level of a permanent and total alteration and the micro-level of momentary breaking of style there is a middle ground—visible when a poet changes a single prominent aspect of style in composing a new volume. We can see such a choice when Lowell, for instance, decides, as he did in *Notebook,* to write a whole new volume in unrhymed sonnet form. As always, such a choice has many causes. Lowell was taking on a new genre, the diary (necessarily composed of short entries and therefore asking for a short form); since days are equal in length, he found it tempting to imitate calendrical form in isometric verses; and Lowell was following (and evoking) his beloved Milton in putting the normally erotic or meditative sonnet to chiefly political use. The choice is also motivated by Lowell's lifelong restless alternation between free verse and metrical verse, between the rhymed and the unrhymed; and it arises from his wish to be loose-limbed in historical description and prophetic in political apothegm, a wish that could be satisfied by the expansive meditation and the couplet-closure available in sonnets.

In looking for three authors in whom I could examine the breaking of style and the forming of a new permanent or temporary stylistic body, I chose Gerard Manley Hopkins as a paradigmatic and famous case from the past whom I could cite to show what I mean by the breaking of style and its perceptual, aesthetic, and moral implications. I could then pass on, with those theoretical points established, to two very different but equally interesting cases in the present—Seamus Heaney, my example of temporary changes of style; and Jorie Graham, my example of how a new stylistic feature can characterize a whole volume.

Hopkins is famous for breaking his style in two: his juvenile poems were followed by a seven-year silence, after which he emerged, in "The Wreck of the Deutschland," as a poet reborn in a new prosody which he called "sprung rhythm." Since prosody is not often written about in terms of its existential meaning—as a cloning of the kinesthetic perceptions of its poet—I thought it useful to consider Hopkins' rupture of his earlier metrics as my example of a totalizing and life-reforming breaking of style.

Because the Irish poet Seamus Heaney's exquisite style, with its fluid modulation from individual poem to individual poem, has been relatively uncommented-upon, while his political attitudes have been much noticed, I decided to look to him as the example of micro-adjustments on the stylistic level. Every poem has of course many micro-levels: phonetic, etymological, prosodic, stanzaic, tonal, grammatical, syntactic, imagistic, dynamic, and so on. I decided to look at grammar in Heaney, since he often foregrounds, in a poem, a particular grammatical "part of speech." This grammatical level of style (now that even students of literature can no longer name or identify the parts of speech) is almost entirely neglected. Yet in defining lyric "atmosphere," it is of crucial importance to be able to give a coherent grammatical and syntactic description of a poem. Nounness, verbness, adjectiveness, and adverbness are all "atmospheres" which help give poems their characteristic "weather," as I hope to show using a few of Heaney's distinctive experiments.

Finally, to represent successive breakings of style visible as a poet changes a single aspect of writing from volume to volume, I have chosen the example of changing lineation in Jorie Graham's three volumes, *Erosion*, *The End of Beauty*, and *Materialism*. Though lineation is one of the micro-levels of style, when one form of lineation dominates a whole volume (as is the case so far with Graham), the aesthetic and moral character of the volume (a macro-level) is thereby signified, in one important way, by that very choice of lineation. Lineation (like prosody and grammar) is a feature of style that often goes unnoticed. It, too, has existential meaning—and as Graham passes from short antiphonal lines to numbered long lines to square "areas" of longlined long sentences, her sense of the poet's task, which changes from volume to volume, is carried precisely (if not solely) by these stylistic changes.

It is distressing, to anyone who cares for and respects the concentrated intellectual and imaginative work that goes into a successful poem, to see how rarely that intense (if instinctive) labor is perceived, remarked on, and appreciated. It is even more distressing—given the human perceptual, aesthetic, and moral signals conveyed (as I hope to show) by such elements as prosody, grammar, and lineation—that most contemporary interpretations of poetry never mention such things, or, if they do, it is to register them factually rather than to deduce their human import. The forgettable writers of verse do not experiment with style in any coherent or strenuous way; they adopt the generic style of their era and, like "the mob of gentlemen who wrote with ease" (the phrase is Pope's), repeat themselves in it. The three writers I take up here are led to experiment not only by their consciousness of the fluidity and adaptability of language and form, but also by their own moral and intellectual and aesthetic changes over time.

Poets are often praised for insight or wisdom, and they may, as persons and as writers, exhibit those qualities; but Pope came nearer to the truth in his clear-eyed remark that what we find in poetry is "What oft was thought, but ne'er so well expressed." Neither poets nor their readers like to admit that poems enunciate "What oft was thought." Yet poets are not primarily original thinkers; they, like other intellectuals, generally think with (and against) the available intellectual categories of their epoch. Philosophers, rather than poets, invent the thought of their epoch. What poets (along with other artists) invent is the *style* of their epoch, which corresponds to, and records, the feelings felt in their epoch. They do this through their gifts of expressiveness; and it is in homage to those gifts, so often slighted in their material form, that I present these brief observations—on the expressiveness of prosody broken and re-formed between youth and maturity by Hopkins; on the expressiveness of grammar broken and re-formed poem by poem by Heaney; and on the expressiveness of lineation broken and re-formed, volume after volume, by Graham.

Gerard Manley Hopkins and Sprung Rhythm

• • •

My first example of the joys and risks in the breaking of style is the invention of sprung rhythm by the Victorian poet Gerard Manley Hopkins (1844–1889), who, as is well known, wrote almost no poetry for seven years after he became a Jesuit, thinking it incompatible with his vocation. But when his superior suggested that someone should write an elegy for the five German Franciscan nuns who were among those drowned when a storm wrecked their ship, the *Deutschland,* Hopkins set to work, embodying in his elegiac ode "The Wreck of the Deutschland" (1876) the new rhythm that had been silently declaring itself to him. The ode sounded remarkably unlike the verse Hopkins had composed in his twenties, and he felt compelled to write a theoretical account of his new prosody, referring to it as "sprung" rhythm. The basic principles of sprung rhythm are that only accentual stresses count in the metrics of a line, and that all poetic feet begin with a stressed syllable. That initial stressed syllable can be followed by one unstressed syllable, or two, or three, or none. I want to describe this rhythm, to suggest why Hopkins invented it (or rather, used it more than anyone else had done), and why he sometimes did *not* use it. It corresponded to his most fundamental intuition of the beautiful—that the beautiful was dangerous, irregular, and binary.

In practice, the most striking effect of sprung rhythm (which Hopkins derived from a mixture of Greek and Anglo-Saxon practice) is to electrify the line with spondees, often emphasized by alliteration and assonance:

> Jésu, héart's líght,
> Jésu, máid's són,
> Whát was the féast fóllowed the níght
> Thou hadst glóry of thís nún?
> (*Poetical Works*, 127)

The other, contrastive feature of sprung rhythm is its frequent lightness, caused by the rapid succession of multiple unstressed syllables:

> lóvely-felícitous Próvidence,
> Fínger of a ténder of, O of a féathery délicacy, the bréast of the
> Máiden could obéy so, be a béll to, ríng of it, and
> Stártle the poor shéep back! is the shípwrack then a hárvest,
> does témpest carry the gráin for thee?
> (127)

This prosodic twoness—stressed march beats versus rapid, tripping, almost liquid footfalls—characterizes all sprung rhythm.

Now the impression given by the two-part Deutschland stanza—four short lines of narrative followed by four longer lines of meditation—also has a twoness about it. In the stanza-discourse, first we are being brisk, and then we become leisurely:

> —On Saturday sailed from Bremen,
> American-outward-bound,
> Take settler and seamen, tell men with women,
> Two hundred souls in the round—

O Father, not under thy feathers nor ever as guessing
The goal was a shoal, of a fourth the doom to be
    drowned;
      Yet *did* the dark side of the bay of thy blessing
Not vault them, the million of rounds of thy mercy not reeve
    even them in?

                                                 (122)

"Pied" or two-part beauty was, for Hopkins, *the* definitive beauty: stressed strength and unstressed featheriness; breathless narrative and arrested meditation; the double-exposure of himself—a male Jesuit in remote prayer—paralleled with a female nun in violent shipwreck. Part I of the ode is about its male speaker's spiritual crisis; Part II is about the tall nun, the heroine who calls out, at the moment of shipwreck, the words closing the Revelation of Saint John, "Oh Christ, Christ, come quickly!" At the climax of Hopkins' ode, the speaker strives to enter the mind of his heroine, and, after several wrong conjectures, feels he intuits the actual meaning of her call—that Christ was to *cure* the extremity where he had cast her. Her confidence (mistaken in the actual event, but correct in its attribution of that curative power to the Christ who calmed the tempest) becomes the guarantee of the speaker's own renewed faith; in an overlap, palimpsest, or double-exposure, her insight becomes his.

The double protagonist is, on the level of plot, the most important piedness of the several piednesses inhabiting Hopkins' ode. Various forms of doubleness and piedness recur through the "Wreck," sometimes innocently but sometimes in a troubled way, prophetic of ethical difficulties to come:

      (O Deutschland, double a desperate name!
         O wórld wíde of its góod!
    But Gertrude, lily, and Luther, are two of a town,
    Chríst's líly, and béast of the wáste wóod:

> From lífe's dáwn it is dráwn dówn,
> Ábel is Cáin's brother and bréasts they have súcked the sáme.)
>
> (124)

This sort of piedness—that of the ethical realm where black-and-white piedness exhibits a damned Luther and a saved Gertrude—is no longer innocent. For the moment, however, a new pied, resurrected body for the name "Deutschland" solves, through the Christ both incarnate and divine, the name's previous undesirable ethical piedness:

> Now burn, new born to the world,
> Double-naturèd name,
> The heaven-flúng, heart-fléshed, máiden-fúrled
> Míracle-in-Máry-of-fláme,
> Mid-numberèd he in three of the thunder-throne!
>
> (128)

The features exhibiting piedness in "The Deutschland"—piedness of rhythm, pledness of stanza-discourse, piedness of male-female plot, a piedness of physical nature (which I will come to shortly), and a troubling piedness of ethics—are the elements of the new Hopkinsian stylistic body which had been seven years in gestation. The masculine fire of inspiration, Hopkins said in his last poem, breathes once and departs, leaving the mind the mother of immortal song:

> Nine months she then, nay years, nine years she long
> Within her wears, bears, cares and combs the same.
>
> (204)

After the emblematic nine years, or, in actuality, seven years, the new body of the new Hopkins poem is brought to birth in "The Deutschland."

What had been the style of Hopkins' "old" stylistic body, seven years earlier? Far from being visibly pied, it was a body in search of bodilessness, of spirituality. Wanting to reflect, in its own verbal substance, what it understood of the substance of the divine, it wanted to lack compositeness. A body formed in imitation of the indivisible divine substance (the young Hopkins thought) needed to be pure, simple, and unvariegated, expressible in a homogeneously invariant rhythm. In 1865, when he was twenty-one, Hopkins wrote a Christmas poem putting off his old Oxford aesthetic self and embracing a new spiritual body of this pure, homogeneous, and invariant sort:

> Moonless darkness stands between.
> Past, the Past, no more be seen!
> But the Bethlehem-star may lead me
> To the sight of Him Who freed me
> From the self that I have been.
> Make me pure, Lord: Thou art holy;
> Make me meek, Lord: Thou wert lowly;
> Now beginning, and alway:
> Now begin, on Christmas day.
>
> (86)

This derivative simplicity does not carry stylistic conviction. Later, in 1876, in an attempt to find variegation even in the simple divine substance, Hopkins fastened on the threeness of the Trinity, "Utterer, Utterèd, Uttering" (137); but the sameness of the root gives the game away: "-er," "-èd," and "-ing," of themselves, are "accidentals" attached to the substantial and invariant etymon "utter." Real variegation has not occurred.

Hopkins had felt it necessary, at twenty-five, to resign himself, in "The Kind Betrothal" (an 1869–70 variant of the 1866 "The Habit of Perfection"), to the complete repudiation of piedness in favor of elected blindness, which itself replaced prelapsarian "simple sight":

> Be shellèd eyes with double dark
> That brings the uncreated light:
> These pièd shows they make their mark,
> Tease, charge, and coil the simple sight.
>
> (91)

Even in the unpied, pure, homogeneous, and regular iambic stylistic body of the young Hopkins, however, little shoots of heterogeneous pied shock had begun to put their heads above ground. In 1864, when he was twenty, Hopkins had written his first version of a poem on the early Christian martyr Saint Dorothea. The original version of the poem is written in shockless iambics:

> I bear a basket lined with grass;
> I am so light, I am so fair,
> That men must wonder as I pass
> And at the basket that I bear.
>
> (56)

Four years later, in a revised version, we can see Hopkins' first timid attempt to find a new stylistic body; the iambs stiffen into trochees, and every so often the characteristic sprung spondee, brought to our attention by Hopkins' stress-marks on "so" and "basket," condenses utterance and calls a halt to metrical evenness:

> I bear a basket lined with grass.
> I am só light and fair

Men must start to see me pass
And the básket I bear.

(57)

But is it enough to say "spondee" and think we have described
the Hopkinsian aesthetic effect? What these and the far more
developed later spondees represent, in mimetic terms, is a universe
of continual irregular shocks, in which the normal expectable
motions of physical law—from peaceable alternations of day and
night to reassuringly identical repetitions of iambs—have been
replaced by an unpredictable series of unforeseen impulses. Or,
putting the mimesis psychologically instead of cosmically, one
could say that the spondees represent the impressions of a poet
who receives the stimuli of daily life as a series of unforeseeable
and unsettling assaults. The regular measures of ordinary verse
simply did not seem to Hopkins to represent the felt texture of
his experience, which was "counter, original, spare, strange" (144).
And the first duty of any poet is to reconfigure felt experience in
an analogical rhythm—prosodic, syntactic, or structural.

Hopkins' shocks are those of an assaultive inscape—almost
always a contrastive inscape of twoness—which provokes a resul-
tant affective instress; and these shocks arrive through the senses.
After the sullen dullness of the English winter, for example, Hop-
kins reacted with what was almost a pathology of ecstasy to the
first bright day:

> For how to the heart's cheering
> The down-dugged ground-hugged grey
> Hovers off, the jay-blue heavens appearing
> Of pied and peeled May!
> Blue-beating and hoary-glow height; or night, still
> higher,

With bélled fire and the móth-soft Mílky Wáy.
What bý your méasure is the héaven of desíre,
The tréasure never éyesight gót, nor was éver guessed whát
for the héaring?

(126)

Because "the heaven of desire" for Hopkins, in order to match his own sense of beauty, had to be variegated, his images for it are always those of pied configurations—blue and white, like the May sky in daytime, or fiery-against-black, like the night sky. For this reason, "Pied Beauty," written when Hopkins was thirty-three (1877, dated by Hopkins), is so important a poem for his aesthetic, reconciling, as it does, the unicity of God with the variety of the natural universe:

Glóry be to God for dappled things—
    For skies of couple-colour as a brinded cow;
        For rose-moles all in stipple upon trout that swim;
Fresh-firecoal chestnut-fálls; fínches' wings;
    Lándscape plotted and pieced—fold, fallow, and plough;
        And áll trádes, their gear and tackle and trim.

Áll things counter, original, spáre, stránge;
    Whatever is fickle, frecklèd (who knows how?)
        With swíft, slów; sweet, sóūr; adázzle, dím;
He fathers-forth whose beauty is pást chánge:
                                        Práise hím.

(144)

The Plotinian one-in-many, Christianized into the fathering crea-tivity of God displaying itself in the universe, was Hopkins' first figure of theological confirmation for piedness, justifying his own delight in variation. (There are, however, no human beings pre-sent in "Pied Beauty.") In the "octave" of this "curtal sonnet,"

Hopkins conceives of piedness as, first, what we would call a relation of figure and ground, which he usually called "dapple": repetitions of one color against a background of another color, like "rose-moles all in stipple upon trout that swim" or white clouds on a blue sky. Or piedness could be alternating patches of two or more equal colors, in which neither is field, neither ground—like fields bearing different crops, "landscape plotted and pieced." Or piedness could be generous variety under a single rubric—the "gear and tackle and trim" of any given trade.

In the "sestet" of "Pied Beauty," however, Hopkins' definition of piedness becomes, almost insensibly, more and more a question of direct opposition, of things "counter": and some of his adjectives ("fickle," "freckled") and adjectival nouns ("sour," "dim") begin to shade over into a moral register. The varied begins to suggest the unreliable, the dappled begins to approach the maculate, the relishable includes the vinegary, and the ecstatic dazzle can blur into the ambiguous. My explicitness exaggerates, of course, since it is only with hindsight that one is tempted to read "Pied Beauty" in this way; yet one cannot refrain from doing so, once one has read "Spelt from Sibyl's Leaves," in which things "counter" come hideously down to the ethical categories of "bláck, white; | ríght, wrong" (191).

I will arrive eventually at "Spelt from Sibyl's Leaves," but for the moment I want to describe Hopkins' new body of style as it is articulated in "Pied Beauty" (144). Hopkins' ecstatic *thought* is voiced in his initial easy and regular trochees: "Glory be to God for dappled things." The subsequent shocks of physical *sensation,* though, have to be conveyed by the spondees I have already mentioned, or else by strong stresses separated by "unimportant" swallowed sounds in the unstressed syllables. Hopkins mentioned, in his description of "Pied Beauty" to Robert Bridges, this tendency of unstressed syllables to disappear (*Letters,* 156). According to Hopkins' own directions in the letter, we are to scan "couple-colour" not as two trochees but as a spondee followed by the unstressed syllable "our": "cóup(le) cólour." The same deletion is made in "brinded cow," where we read "brínd(ed)ców." In each case, the negligible unstressed syllable between two stressed syllables is prosodically, in Hopkins' scheme, nonexistent.*

Thus, there are far more "spondees" in Hopkins than an ordinary glance at the page (in which unstressed syllables are normally registered as metrically present) would suggest. His mature style is one that forcibly embodies the inscape-assaults that he received, instressed as metrical shocks. When ecstasy is in question, the "squeezing out" of the interstices between shocks is a means of maximizing rapture, as in the sestet of "The Windhover":

> Brute beauty and valour and act, oh, air, pride, plŭme, here
> Buckle! AND. . . .
>
> (144)

This is to be read, orally, obeying Hopkins' own marked directions—stresses, sforzandos, and elisions—as,

> Brute béaut(y and) vál(our and) áct (oh, air) príde plŭme (here)
> Búck(le)! ÁND. . . .

*Hopkins took great care to make his unstressed syllables, in such cases, negligible ones, semantically speaking: the *l* of "couple" is present in "colour" to replace, so to speak, the *l* that is almost dropped as we say "coup(le)"; and the *d* of the initial "brind-" in "brind(ed)" does duty for the one we drop before we say "cow." To represent the pause that replaced the dropped syllable, Hopkins used a "great colon" between the two words; as he said in the letter cited above about the similar phrase "dápp(led) things," "This last syllable [e.g., of 'dappled'] is not so much a syllable by itself as strengthens the one before it, so that the true scansion is—'dappled : things' etc." Hopkins even inserted a "great colon" in the middle of some true spondees in "Pied Beauty" (e.g., "past : change" and "Praise : him") to emphasize the pause or shock caused by the two stressed words forcibly jammed up against each other.

The "stairstep" quality of the lines, read as Hopkins accented them, mounts at its peak to its capitalized enactment of ecstatic inventory. But when the shocks undergone are not ecstatic but painful ones, it is agony that is made even more intense by the "squeezing out" of whatever unstressed interstices might have offered relief and respite: the "blue-bleak embers" of "The Wind-hover" are said to "Fall, gáll themsélves, (and) gásh góld-ver-míl(ion)."

The mature body of Hopkins' style is thus designed to be capable of rendering psychic shock, both ecstatic and painful, and it intensifies its fundamental spondaic crush by extreme syntactic compression, as well as by alliterating or assonating the spondaic syllables, as in "fall/gall/gash." Hopkins frequently wants to condense experience as much as possible, compressing, for example, the regular sonnet into "curtal" brevity, while preserving (in his exaggerated carefulness) the exact proportions of the regular sonnet in its reduced "curtal" form.* Hopkins' condensation of the sonnet form to ten and a half lines in "Pied Beauty" matches not only his syntactic condensation and his condensation of metrical movement into spondees but also his condensation of the world's disturbing variety into intelligible antithetical form ("swift, slow; sweet, sour; adazzle, dim"). For the moment, Hopkins is telling us—through the stylistic body in which his rendition of the world moves—that though the world appears to him infinitely various, it is ultimately intelligible, not through the logically intelligible world of philosophy, nor through the recursively intelligible world of physics, but rather through the unpredictably intelligible world of antithetical sensation, alternately rapturous and painful. As the shocks of original sensation crowd thick and fast on one another, they are rapidly compressed by Hopkins'

*This can only be expressed fractionally, since its 6 : 4½ shape is really equal, as Hopkins was at pains to point out in his "Author's Preface on Rhythm" (*Poetical Works*, 117), to 12/2 : 9/2. Its ratio 12 : 9 matches the regular sonnet's proportion of 4 : 3.

ecstatically instressing mind into a condensation of their original arrival.

The original shocks of sensual perception are invariably distilled by the sestet of a Hopkins sonnet to a curtailed version of themselves, a version which is no longer sensuous but rather moral and intellectual—what we might call a second-order instressing. I have no doubt that this progressive condensation is the structural equivalent of what went on, seriatim, in Hopkins' immensely sensual receptive apparatus and his energetic intellectual apparatus. And therefore the critics who see the sonnets "spoiled" by the "tacking-on" of a moral after a brilliant sensuous rendition of the world fail to recognize Hopkins' compulsion, as an artist, to render accurately and fully his secondary interior intellectual process, as well as his primary sensuous process. Receive expansively and then concentrate mentally; spread receptively and then hammer sensation into intellectual shape; this was the law of Hopkins' entire being. In sensuous and sensual matters, the spreading-out came first, as he became an absorptive medium to the shocks of being; and the contracting wave came second, as he then concentrated himself into a processor and shaper of what he had received. In narrative matters, though, the contracting came first (as in the swift telling of the plot of the "Deutschland") and the stanzaic expansiveness followed, as meditation dilated on what a prior event had offered.

This was all a great lyric advance on Hopkins' part—to move away from his youthful focus on the univocal and indivisible substance of an invisible deity and a virtuous soul, embodied in too-fluent and stylistically homogeneous stanzas. He moved instead toward the divinely fathered and contrastively varied accidents of the world, insisted on an intellectual as well as sensuous account of his own responses, and created a stanzaic mimesis which would slight neither his unequaled expansive receptivity toward sensuous shock nor his intense contractive intellectual being.

Hopkins' first stylistic attempt at rendering the variety of his experience, restricting itself in "Pied Beauty" to the world of nature, was successful. But his second attempt to incorporate the variety of the world was far more problematic: this was his attempt to justify his response to human bodies, chiefly male bodies. His relishing eye now dwelt not only on clouds and landscapes, but on "world's loveliest, men's selves" (183). And that beauty, as he knew and said, was even more dangerous than the distracting beauty of nature. His focus on God as the father of the beauty of nonhuman nature had enabled the composition of "Pied Beauty," from which, as I have said, human beauty was carefully excluded. And the stylistic body of that poem—radically condensed, shock-filled, skirting the dangerous in its adjectives but thematically serene in the initial trochees of its "Glory be to God for dappled things"—was entirely adequate to Hopkins' ecstatic sensuous and intellectual reception of nonhuman beauty. The moral danger came with the instress of "mortal beauty," and Hopkins explored that ethical danger in many poems, thematically in the sonnet "To what serves Mortal Beauty?" and visually in poems on Felix Randal, Harry Ploughman, and the Bugler Boy. It was only in contemplating human beauty that he faced what the aesthetic moment, at its most intense, was to him. Theologically speaking, Hopkins' short answer to his sexual arousal before male bodies (that "dancing blood" which he experienced concomitant with aesthetic appreciation) was to say that since Christ became incarnate nothing concerning the flesh is unredeemed. Just as, in "Pied Beauty," God the Father by his dissemination of his unity into varied creation "saves" natural beauty, so God incarnate in Christ "saves" mortal human beauty. Just as natural beauty reveals the being of the Father as it deals out its own being, so mortal beauty, says a sonnet roughly contemporaneous with "Pied Beauty" (Norman MacKenzie conjecturally dates it 1877) deals out the being of Christ incarnate:

As kingfishers catch fire, dragonflies draw flame;
  As tumbled over rim in roundy wells
  Stones ring; like each tucked string tells, each hung bell's
Bow swung finds tongue to fling out broad its name;
Each mortal thing does one thing and the same:
  Deals out that being indoors each one dwells;
  Selves—goes its self; *myself* it speaks and spells,
Crying *What I do is me: for that I came.*

Í say more: the just man justices;
  Keeps gráce: thát keeps all his goings graces;
Ácts in God's eye what in God's éye hè is—

  Chríst. For Christ plays in ten thousand places,
Lovely in limbs, and lovely in eyes not his
  To the Father through the features of men's faces.

(141)

In Hopkins' sonnets on natural beauty, the sensual part of the poem normally occupies the whole octave. Here, however, the sensual has been reduced to the initial four lines, which reproduce delights to eye and ear dealt by "mortal things." This new category, "mortal things," is broad enough to include both nature and man, so that the poem can pass from the physically expressive "selving" of a kingfisher or a stone to the (apparently comparable) ethically expressive "selving" of a just man. The ethical moment is always ranked by Hopkins as uniquely important; and for him it is strictly incomparable, in its supreme and decisive salvific importance, to either the sensuous receptive moment or the formulating intellectual moment, though always arising in conjunction with them. That ethical moment—"the just man justices"—is here "tucked away" between two other parts: the first is a sensuous moment (the flame of dragonflies, the tongue of bells) followed by its intellectual gnomic formula *"What I do is me"*; the second is another sensuous moment, theologically inflected, in which Christ "plays" everywhere, "lovely" in limbs and "lovely" in eyes. Once the just man acts as Christ would, he becomes free to relish the play of a loveliness visible in men's limbs and faces, a sensuous loveliness which Hopkins ascribes, ultimately, to Christ playing in men's limbs.

This thematic structure—by which Hopkins inserts ethical behavior ("justicing") as a bridge from a field of sensuous and linguistic play in the natural world ("selving") to a field of sensuous play in the "lovely limbs" of the human dimension—is an ingenious one, and it allows us to see what, for Hopkins, the full "aesthetic moment" must contain: sensuous relish, intellectual formulation, and ethical value. Hopkins will repudiate this ingenious structure eight years later, when he reconsiders this problem in "To what serves Mortal Beauty?" (1885). But even in its first, "justicing" deployment here, the ethical moment constrains Hopkins' aesthetic, since the later sensuous moment which responds to men's bodies forbids itself any of the joyous particularity of the language earlier used to describe kingfishers, dragonflies, and even stones. The "limbs," "faces," and "features" of men (though qualified as "lovely," and given "shock value" by the alliterative stress of "lovely" and "limb") remain resolutely undescribed in Hopkinsian sensuous language. If the sensual reception of men's bodies were truly "just," it should be able to be fully relished, sensuously and verbally. But when Hopkins gives himself more sensuous room than he does here, the subject of the male body becomes dangerous, and stylistic failure in description betrays the strain: in "Harry Ploughman," the poem tends to fall into sentimental indulgence ("See his wind-lílylócks-láced"); and in "The Bugler's First Communion," metaphor takes on such unconscious sexual analogy that a psychoanalytic reading finds it almost risible (the bugler boy "to all I teach / Yields ténder as a púshed péach").

When, eight years after "As kingfishers catch fire," Hopkins, now forty-one, writes "To what serves Mortal Beauty?" (182) he faces up to, and states, the fact of the "dancing blood" of sexual arousal (which goes unmentioned in his poems about the blacksmith, the ploughman, and the bugler). He must now devise, if his poem is to be accurate, a poetic dynamic proper to a Christian poet, one capable of an ethically "just" aesthetic description of sexually attractive bodies. What he devises is a "zigzag" structure of the aesthetic moment, in which the ongoing instress of the sensuous relish of bodies is continually monitored and countered by the speaker's shifting of his attention away from bodies to an intellectual, ethical, or theological instress. Instead of postponing the ethical moment to the middle of the poem, as he had in "As kingfishers," Hopkins now opens the poem boldly with his ethical question: "To what serves mortal beauty?"

To what serves mortal beauty I —dangerous; does set danc-
Ing blood—the O-seal-that-so I face, prouder flung the form
Than Purcell tune lets tread to? I See, it does this: keeps warm
Men's wits to the things that are; I what good means—where
    a glance
Master more may than gaze, I gaze out of countenance.
Those lovely lads once, wet-fresh I windfalls of war's storm,
How then should Gregory, a father, I have gleanèd else from
    swarm-
Èd Rome? But God to a nation I dealt that day's dear chance.
To man, that once would worship I block or barren stone,
Our law says: Love what are I love's worthiest, were all
    known;
World's loveliest—men's selves. Self I flashes off frame and
    face.
What do then? how meet beauty? I Merely meet it; own,
Home at heart, heaven's sweet gift; I then leave, let that alone.
Yea, wish that though, wish all, I God's better beauty, grace.

                                    (182–183)

Here, Hopkins can at last allow bits of sensually responsive language their play, feeling free to use for men's bodies the verbs "flash" and "flung," words which belong to that family of monosyllabic verbs (like "catch," "ring," and "fling," in "As kingfishers") which are his hieroglyph for an intermittent pied moment of a flashing against a dark, or a flinging against an immobility, representing sensuous instress felt. He also allows himself to summon up, in terms far more explicit than those used in "As kingfishers," the sexual attractiveness of young men, as he recalls the Angles that Saint Gregory called angels: "Those lovely lads once, wet-fresh windfalls of war's storm." The two alliterative instress-shocks here—"*ló*ve(*ly*) *lá*ds'" and "*wé*t-*frè*sh | *wí*nd*fa*lls"— denote a sensual acknowledgment, "message received." Hopkins' usual sign of especially strong instress is a reference to the delight of both eye and ear: he applies that double sign in the sonnet as he asserts (in his condensed and alliterative diction of pleasurable shock) that the visually relished face should be preserved ("sealed") as it now is, and that its body is even prouder flung, in its motion, than a body moving to a piece of music by Hopkins' favorite composer, Purcell.

This sensuous instressing (which, we must recall, was preceded by the sonnet's opening ethical question of the purpose of mortal beauty) immediately yields to an intellectual justification for human beauty. This turn to the intellect is, I repeat, as authentic a response, in a poet so intellectual as Hopkins, as is sensuous relishing. To what serves mortal beauty?

> See, it does this: keeps warm
> Men's wits to the things that are.

This is beauty's first function—to make men look at the world, at the "things that are," external reality. Hopkins was enough of an Aristotelian, not to mention a Scotist, to think that the physical "things that are" are the ground of intellection. He dares to say even that the beautiful can teach us an important truth about the ethical, which is that the good must be at least as beautiful as the beautiful. Mortal beauty tells us "what good means." This is a powerful and trenchant defense—but Hopkins follows it with a lesson in how to respond to beauty in the guise of a description of beauty's effect. A "glance," he says, may master more than a "gaze." The "glance" is still that of sensuous responsiveness, as we can tell by the "shocks" of the phrase "Mást(er) móre máy." The overlong and embarrassing "gaze" is intellectually disenfranchised, and no continuing pleasurable shocks are ascribed to it in the line. There follow the delightful shocks of the Angles/angels; but they are immediately countered by a set of equal salvific theological shocks: "God to a nation | déalt that dáy's dèar chance." After each instress of the flashes of loveliness, in short, the poem turns to counter that sensuous instress with religious or intellectual exhortation and an accompanying instress of religious perception. After meeting beauty—"Hóme (at heart), héaven's sweet gift"—one must, abstaining, "léave, let thát alóne." The poem ends with an attempt—in its epithet "God's bétt(er) béaut(y)"—to make grace exert an instress as strong as the one represented by the dangerous dance of the blood. By putting grace in a hierarchic continuum under the general rubric "Beauty"—positive mortal beauty, comparative "better beauty" (grace), and the superlative best beauty, God—Hopkins expresses his faith that the ethical can be seen as a comparative degree of the sensuous, even of the sensual. Each is a way station to the divine. They can all, therefore, express their instressing shocks without conflict; and the rule of thumb for the Christian is to pass rapidly—after only a "glance"—from the positive sensuous dimension to the comparative ethical, intellectual, or theological one, and thence to the superlative divine one. Each of the two "higher" degrees, once entered, enables in the poet a sinless brief return to the sensual "dancing blood."

The zigzag dynamic of recurrent attention from flesh to spirit that structures "To what serves Mortal Beauty?" is undeniably an anxious complication of the "easier" earlier structure by which a long and unembarrassed sensuous instress of a starlight night or a spring landscape was concluded by a bringing home of its intellectual, ethical, or theological significance. Hopkins' new zigzag stylistic body, invented to deal with the threat that looking at male beauty posed to his spiritual equilibrium, is more nervous and fluctuating than his younger stylistic body, which contended only with nonhuman physical nature. But the new articulation of the stylistic body has found a way of enlisting male beauty into a consonant Platonic hierarchy of beauty reaching from sensuous glance to theological grace and, ultimately, to the divine realm of God himself. Each plane of the hierarchy can allow itself the sprung rhythm of rapture.

There exists in Hopkins' work an alternate ethical formulation of male beauty in which Christ as hero (rather than Christ as archetype of human beauty) justifies Hopkins' admiration for the soldier, as even Christ, viewing the soldier's heroism, "néeds | his néck must fáll on, kíss, / And cry 'O Christ-done deed!'" Beauty of action rather than beauty of countenance is here the object of attention. Yet Hopkins deduces from the "smart" appearance without, that soldiers have an admirable "sterling" self within, though he knows that this is, intellectually speaking, a faulty and feigning move of the fancy:

> the héart,
> Since, proud, it calls the calling | manly, gives a guess
> That, hopes that, mákesbelieve, | the men must be no less;
> It fáncies; ít deems; déars | the ártist áfter his árt;
> So feigns it finds as sterling | all as all is smart.
>
> (184)

For Hopkins, the rift between the smart appearance and the sterling interior, the beautiful face and the ethical justicing, is

always threatening to deepen and widen, with disruptive conse-
quences for his precariously achieved stylistic body.

Why did Hopkins not use sprung rhythm in certain poems
written after he had invented it? To answer this question, we must
look, briefly, at a pure prelapsarian "aesthetic" moment, one into
which the ethical and the theological do not enter; it shows
Hopkins exalted in a completely undangerous way. One June
night in 1876 (as Hopkins tells the story in "Moonrise"), he awoke
in the early hours of the morning and saw the waning moon rising
from behind a dark mountain. The moon, luminous but lustreless
against the white midsummer dawn, had not yet completely de-
tached itself from the silhouetted darkness of the mountain. Star-
tled gently from drowsiness by the sight, Hopkins found himself
open-eyed; and he writes, in perfectly regular heptameter:

> I awoke in the Midsummer not-to-call night, | in the white
>   and the walk of the morning:
> The móon, dwíndled and thínned to the frínge | of a
>   fingernail héld to the cándle,
> Or páring of páradisáïcal frúit, | lóvely in wáning but
>   lústreless,
> Stepped from the stool, drew back from the barrow, | of dark
>   Maenefa the mountain;
> A cusp still clasped him, a fluke yet fanged him, | entangled
>   him, not quit utterly.
> This was the prized, the desirable sight, | unsought, presented
>   so easily,
> Parted me leaf and leaf, divided me, | eyelid and eyelid of
>   slumber.

(131)

The awakened poet sees not "a" prized sight, not "a" desirable
sight, but "the" sight desirable and prized. This is Hopkins'

paradigmatic description of the *un*dangerous aesthetic moment of pure sensuousness as he knows it, the "heaven of desire" achieved. What are the ingredients of this moment, and what do these ingredients produce in the way of a stylistic body?

The first ingredient of the perfect aesthetic moment is its spontaneity: the sight was unsought and it came without effort, it was "presented so easily." The second ingredient is unexpectedness of gestalt: since the night sky in North Wales never becomes entirely dark in midsummer, the moon presents an unusual aspect: luminosity without lustrousness. The poet, so assiduous in his observation of nature, has never before seen this phenomenon—late moonrise in "white" midsummer. The third necessary ingredient is piedness, contrast: a feminized thinnest of male moons, "lovely in waning," is set against the most massive of earth-forms, "dark Maenefa the mountain." The fourth ingredient of the perfect aesthetic moment is dynamic tension: this is produced here by the threatening gesture of the cusps and flukes of the mountain, unwilling to release the lunar body. The "entangl[ing]" of moon and mountain, unexpectedly glimpsed against the unusual white sky, causes the opening of the poet's selfhood to the sight, dividing a "leaf" of the self to the left, another "leaf" to the right, and making both eyelids open.

Now what stylistic body incarnates this innocent moment? In the first place, the dimensions of the poem are self-consciously "perfect," constructed on the heavenly number seven—the poem is seven beats across and seven lines long. (Though Hopkins scanned sprung rhythm with the ictus of the foot always in the first syllabic position, a conventional scansion of this poem would begin not with dactyls but with lulling anapests: "I awoke / in the Mid- / summmer not / to call night / in the white / and the walk / of the morn- / ing.") The only significant pause comes at the end of each line. The little aesthetic shocks include two spondees ("moon, dwind-" and "fruit, love-") each of which is "softened" by a medial comma. Except for "moon" and "fruit," each ictus is followed by a multitude of ravishing little accessory syllables: The moon is "*dwínd(led* and) th*ínn(ed* to the) *ftín(*ge of a) *fíng(*er*n*ail) hé*ld* (to the) cá*nd(le*)." Nothing here resembles the continuously spondaic "swift, slow; sweet, sour; adazzle, dim" of "Pied Beauty." Though in many poems Hopkins relishes the shock of contrast, here, in "Moonrise," for the sheer relaxed and sinless appreciation of beauty, the even chromatism representing intelligible perceptual continuity is the source of pleasure. Hopkins' ideal of the sinless apprehension of beauty, seen in the beginning of "Spelt from Sibyl's Leaves," is not shock but rather an almost imperceptible chromatic modulation: "Earnest, earthless, equal, attuneable, vaulty, voluminous"—and then the spell breaks with the threatening word "stupendous." In "Sibyl's Leaves," the noun that all these adjectives modify is "evening," and one can see them gradually working up to "evening" in their chromatic succession of *e*'s and *n*'s and *v*'s. The line "should" have read "Earnest, earthless, etc. . . . voluminous evening." "Stupendous" breaks in (as its initial harsh consonants and its plosive mar the chromatism) like the sound of the last trump, the "Tuba mirum" of the *Dies Irae*. "Óur night whélms, whélms, ánd will énd us," say the later spondees of the sonnet, also destroying chromatism.

"Moonrise" has no such spondaic menace. Its steady lulling rhythms continue to the end. Its two mild shocks are gentle, not rude. In its unsinful and unthreatening self-presentation, the tableau is prelapsarian; the human fingernail and the paradisal fruit meet without strain in the image of the moon, as though the human, the celestial, and the cosmological were all analogues of one another. The skyscape is still pied—moon and mountain—but both the moon's power to "[step] from the stool, [draw] back from the barrow" of dark Maenefa's dragon-fangs and cusps, and the knowledge that soon the moon will be entirely free, "quit utterly" after the "still" and "yet" of this moment expire, act to reassure us of the final ascendancy of light over darkness, of loveliness over the dragon's hold. Hopkins' intellectual editorial-izing—"This was the prized, the desirable sight"—in the penul-timate line, which reflects on the trance represented in the last words of the poem, says, "I have seen, at least once, the shape of desired beauty." But the editorializing is not permitted to close the poem, as it would have done were this a poem that drew sensual rapture into an intellectual grasp, as Hopkins' early son-nets do. A rapture which is not threatening, like moonrise, will allow, it is true, the penetration of its visual ecstasy by the cate-gorizing intellect—"This was the prized, the desirable sight"—and it will even allow, *pari passu* with its sensuous description, a metaphorical glimpse of a theological archetype (here paradisal fruit set against a glimpse of an equally theological demonic dragon with flukes and fangs, jealous of light). But after these intellectual and metaphorical excursions, this poem can end (be-cause the object of its gaze is ethically neutral and the moment of its gaze—nighttime—is one not claimed by priestly obligation) with the trance of the poet, abed, awake, enthralled, divided leaf from leaf in a receptive and enraptured state. Here, there is none of the nervous back-and-forth movement from stolen glance to thought to stolen glance to theology that we saw prompted by male bodies in "To what serves Mortal Beauty?" The solacing rhythms and the "perfect-number" symmetry of "Moonrise"; its gentle unspondaic aesthetic responsiveness; its peaceable inter-twining of the visual, the theological, and the intellectual; and finally its cessation in rapt sensuous trance rather than in stern intellectual or ethical thought: all of these point to what the stylistic body of the untroubled Hopkinsian self "ought" to be. A reader aware of the ravaged stylistic body of Hopkins' later poems of torture feels a pang when encountering the symmet-rical, untortured, "innocent" metrical and linguistic body of this poem.

We must here come, by contrast, to the tortured body of "Spelt from Sibyl's Leaves." Something terrible has now happened to Hopkins' early impulse, visible in sprung rhythm and in "curtal" sonnets alike, to condense expression to its most compressed form. In a fragment written when he was twenty-one, Hopkins had, through a dramatic persona, announced his poetics of pruning (derived perhaps from Herbert's "Paradise"):

> 'Boughs being pruned, birds preenèd, show more fair;
>> To grace them spires are shaped with corner squinches;
> Enrichèd posts are chamfer'd; everywhere
>> He heightens worth who guardedly diminishes.'

(68)

A good deal of Hopkins' work sprang from this premise—that one should get rid of unnecessary words in a line, cram together sensations, skip rapidly over unstressed syllables, invent gnomic images, make rapid clipped epigrams like "Worst will the best." This is (though from a most unathletic man) an athlete's poetics, where the most economical energy of motion is both the most effective and the most beautiful. A different aspect of Hopkins' poetics—its potential for the expansive and relaxed—is, as we have seen, put to use in moments of repose and delectation, as in "Moonrise."

But in the tragic aggregation of experience, a poetics of pruning and paring will not suffice alone, any more than will a poetics of relaxed sensuous repose. Toward the end of his life, Hopkins writes a group of gigantic sonnets, of which the visibly longest, "That Nature is a Heraclitean Fire and of the comfort of the Resurrection" (197–198) spreads *across* the page in explosive hexameter lines (running to fifteen or more syllables apiece) and hurls itself *down* the page in twenty-four such lines:

Cloud-puffball, torn tufts, tossed pillows │ flaunt forth, then
   chevy on an air-
Built thoroughfare: heaven-roysterers, in gay-gangs │ they
   throng; they glitter in marches.
Down roughcast, down dazzling whitewash, │ wherever an
   elm arches,
Shivelights and shadowtackle ín long │ lashes lace, lance, and
   pair.
Delightfully the bright wind boisterous │ ropes, wrestles, beats
   earth bare
Of yestertempest's creases; │ in pool and rutpeel parches
Squandering ooze to squeezed │ dough, crúst, dust; stánches,
   stárches
Squadroned masks and manmarks │ treadmire toil there
Fóotfretted in it. Million-fuelèd, │ nature's bonfire burns on.
But quench her bonniest, dearest │ to her, her clearest-selvèd
   spark
Mán, how fást his firedint, │ his mark on mind, is gone!
Bóth áre in an únfáthómablè, │ áll is in an enórmous dárk
Drowned. O pity and indig │ nation! Manshape, that shone
Sheer off, disseveral, a star, │ death blots black out; nor mark
               Is ány of him át áll so stárk
But vastness blurs and time │ beats level. Enough! the
   Resurrection,
A héart's-clarion! Awáy grief's gásping, │ joyless days,
   dejection.
               Across my foundering deck shone
A beacon, an eternal beam. │ Flesh fade, and mortal trash
Fáll to the resíduary worm; │ world's wildfire, leave but ash:
               In a flash, at a trumpet crash,
I am all at once what Christ is, │ since he was what I am, and
Thís Jack, jóke, poor pótsherd, │ patch, matchwood, immortal
   diamond,
               Is immortal diamond.

This "sonnet" begins with a conventional Petrarchan octave, but then prolongs itself into a sixteen-line "sestet," which includes four short trimeter "outrides." (I place the outrides in parentheses in the following rhyme scheme.) This "sestet"—rhyming cdcdcd(d)cc(c)ee(e)ff(f)—has added four "extra" rhyming lines in "cd" to the original Petrarchan sestet, and has then appended a "coda" of six more lines (adding the new "e" and "f" rhymes). What does such a stylistic body mean? It makes one think of a science-fiction movie in which a creature is fed some nutriment which makes it elongate its original limbs and sprout extra ones to boot. Yet it is not so much (to continue the metaphor) that the original limbs here "elongate" themselves; rather, they twin or triple themselves. In this poem, nothing can be said once. If there are clouds, they evolve into triple clouds—"cloud-puffball, torn tufts, tossed pillows." If they "throng," their action must be further specified: they "glitter in marches." The wind "ropes, wrestles, beats earth bare." Yesterday's mud turns to "squeezed dough, crust, dust." The metaphorically foundering ship of the poet is illumined by "a beacon, an eternal beam." Mortality is twice conceded: "Flesh fade, and mortal trash / Fall to the residuary worm." Judgment day arrives to both eye and ear: "In a flash, at a trumpet crash." Is not a beacon self-evidently a beam? Is not the fading of flesh necessarily the worms' banquet? Why is everything said twice or thrice, made into a twin or triplet of itself?

What is all this approximated tautology? How can it be issuing from Hopkins, our master of the pruned and the pared? We can understand this "x≈x" body of "Heraclitean Fire" (over which I must pass very lightly in order to reach "Spelt from Sibyl's Leaves") only when we see where the approximational tautologies (such as dust/crust or beacon/beam) converge into "real" ones (x = x). The statement "I am all at once what Christ is, since he was what I am" is the first of the "real" tautologies, a chiasmus that is not quite a chiasmus because of the nonidentity of tenses. "I am : Christ *is* :: he *was* : I am." It almost passes muster, but the poet is not quite the post-Resurrection discarnate Christ. The last tautology, the most total one, is the most daring: the creeping chromatism of "This Jack, joke, poor potsherd, patch, matchwood," is "violated" by the last phrase of the series, *"immortal diamond,"* where we might expect a chromatic approximation— "patch, matchwood, *mortal wretch*." The astonishing final total tautology "immortal diamond, / Is immortal diamond" reveals the reason-for-being of all the earlier approximate tautologies of the stylistic "body" of the poem. By means of Christ's Resurrection, the image and likeness of God in which human beings were originally created, but which has been distorted and marred by sin, is restored to its original identity, to immortal beauty. The long effortful chromatic synonymy of earthly existence—as the fallen sinner, by his imitation of Christ, tries asymptotically to regain perfect tautology—ceases in the identity-equation of redemption. The linguistic symbol of redemption is perfect verbal tautology, as human immortal diamond is one with Christ as immortal diamond. Tautology is the rhetorical mimesis of the restored new Adam seen by Hopkins as the goal of the Christian life; but this redemption, though phrased in the present tense following on the past ("Across my foundering deck *shone* / A beacon . . . / I *am* all at once what Christ is . . . and / This Jack . . . immortal diamond, / *Is* immortal diamond") is of course declared in the present tense of prophetic faith rather than in the present tense of experience. The nagging chromatism of approximational synonymy remains the mark of the experiential: the true tautological is granted by belief alone. The aesthetic moment of brightness after storm can now include the ethically perfect moment of "justicing" only in the envisaged future of salvation.

"Spelt from Sibyl's Leaves," written two years before "Heraclitean Fire," foresaw the eventual disappearance, on the Last Day, of the verbally formulated aesthetic moment which can include, even if with strain, the sensuous, the ethical, and the theological in one. In "Sibyl's Leaves," the speaker faces squarely

an ethical realm harshly denuded of the beautiful. Hopkins told
his friend Robert Bridges that this fourteen-line poem was the
"longest sonnet ever made," and when Bridges reminded him of
earlier sonnets (Milton's) with codas, he answered, "I mean to
enclose my long sonnet, the longest, I still say, ever made; longest
by its own proper length, namely by the length of its lines; for
anything can be made long by eking, by tacking, by trains, tails,
and flounces" (*Letters*, 246). (Two years later, Hopkins would be
quite content to tack his own tails and flounces on "Heraclitean
Fire.") "Sibyl's Leaves" remains strictly within fourteen lines; yet,
since Hopkins was undergoing his compulsion to strain the en-
forced bounds of the sonnet to their utmost, he expanded the
width of the line from the conventional pentameter to eight spun-
out and racked beats. The poem, occurring as evening "strains to
be" a vast "hearse-of-all" night is a heartbroken elegy for pied
beauty, sung while a "double dark" closes in:

Earnest, earthless, equal, attuneable, | vaulty, voluminous, . . .
    stupendous
Evening strains to be tíme's vást, | womb-of-all, home-of-all,
    hearse-of-all night.
Her fond yellow hornlight wound to the west, | her wild
    hollow hoarlight hung to the height
Waste; her earliest stars, earlstars, | stárs principal, overbend
    us,
Fíre-féaturing héaven. For éarth | her béing has unbóund; her
    dápple is at énd, as-
Tray or aswarm, all throughther, in throngs; | self ín self
    stéepèd and páshed—qúite
Disremembering, dísmémbering | áll now. Heart, you round
    me right
With: Óur évening is óver us; óur night | whélms, whélms,
    ánd will énd us.

Only the beakleaved boughs dragonish | damask the
   tool-smooth bleak light; black,
Ever so black on it. Óur tale, Ó óur oracle! | Lét life, wáned,
   ah lét life wínd
Off hér once skéined stained véined varíety | upon, áll on twó
   spools; párt, pen, páck
Now her áll in twó flocks, twó folds—bláck, white; | ríght,
   wrong; réckon but, réck but, mínd
But thése two; wáre of a wórld where bút these | twó tell,
   éach off the óther; of a ráck
Where, selfwrung, selfstrung, sheathe- and shelterless, |
   thóughts agaínst thoughts ín groans grínd.

                                                          (190–191)

A strange tautological synonymy seems to be at work here, too,
but it is distressingly self-querying. Is it "astray" or "aswarm" one
should say? Is it (yet more frightening) "disremembering" or
(horrible to think) "dismembering"? An apocalyptic tautology
insisting on the total end of variety is here as well: "Our night |
whelms, whelms, and will end us." "Bleak" turns to "black" and
then can only repeat itself in intensified tautologous form—"ever
so black." "Reckon but" repeats itself in broken tautologous
cadence—"reck but."
   If, for the style of "Heraclitean Fire," the metaphor that comes
to mind is that of a body synonymously almost twinning itself in
an effort to find its "true" image, which—in the final twinning,
of tautologous identity rather than synonymy—turns out to be
the image of the incarnate and redemptive Christ, then the meta-
phor that comes to mind for "Sibyl's Leaves" is that of a body
disintegrating into ever more shapeless fragments as each part
entropically comes to resemble every other fragmented member.
As the Sibyl's book is unbound, the original delightful varieties
of piedness succumb, one after the other, to total blackness. Is

any piedness left? The piedness of sprung rhythm remains: of what is its twoness now the moral sign?

The poem, after posing the question of natural piedness through its octave, performs in the sestet an astonishing involution of its former distressed gaze, the gaze that was, in the twilight, bent on a piedness that seemed to be disappearing. Yes, there is still piedness, the sestet asserts, but it is not for long an *exterior* one; after the fading of the last visual piedness—the damascene blades of the leaves against the steely light—the material world will become totally black. The only piedness left then will be the *interior*, ethical, and eschatological one of the Ignatian choice of life—"bláck, white; ríght, wrong." The poem ends on the rack of that ethical choice; but Hopkins bypasses even the exterior visual metaphor for the piedness of evil and good, "bláck, white," in favor of his ever more interior moral instress of that choice as "ríght, wrong." In the final deathly tautology of the poem, "thóughts agaínst thoughts ín groans grínd." The good thoughts, the evil thoughts, the black thoughts, the white thoughts, are all thoughts, thoughts, and more thoughts grinding against each other in groans, groans, and more groans. "We hear our hearts grate on themselves: it kills / To bruise them dearer," Hopkins had written in a sonnet on Patience. It is the sound of that tautologous and undifferentiated self-grating, rather than either visual or ethical piedness, that we last perceive in "Sibyl's Leaves," and its only possible consequence is the bruising and bruised death of mind and heart alike on the rack of conscience. The only echo of piedness left is the adjunct sounds distinguishing the two forms of the consonant cluster *g-r-n* into "groans" and "grind."

The intolerably long lines of "Sibyl's Leaves," with their recurrent spondaic shocks, are responsible for the chief aesthetic impression left by the poem: the horrifying leisureliness of the dismemberment of the self. A rapid extinction might not qualify as torture; but the menacing gradual dismemberment of the sestet surely does. The relentless spondees—"whélms, whélms"—and the feet in which two monosyllables receive almost equal stress—"twó flocks, twó folds—bláck, white; I ríght, wrong; réck(on) but, réck but, mínd / But thése two"—culminate in the final rasping half-line "thóughts agaínst thoughts ín groans grínd." To cut sentences up monosyllabically in this way—as though it were no longer possible to make what in music would be called a legato phrase—is to enact, through sprung rhythm and its monotonous monosyllabic rocking to-and-fro movement, the dismembered body and the disremembering word. As he here represents his most despairing instress of the world, Hopkins still must, to be truthful to his own sense of piedness, suspend himself in interior ethical contrast, the final choice of white rightness as yet unmade. One can make that final choice only at the unmaking of both word and world at the precise moment of death.

The unique importance, for Hopkins, of the ethical realm is its eventual menace to the realm of the pied postlapsarian beautiful as he understood it. His dismembered body is his final sacrifice of sensuous responsiveness to an ethical priority which was his inmost given:

> Man lives that list, that leaning in the will
> No wisdom can forecast by gauge or guess,
> The selfless self of self, most strange, most
>   still,
> Fast furled and all foredrawn to No or Yes.
>
> (192)

Unable to know whether he would answer No or Yes with his last breath—since no wisdom can forecast it—Hopkins strained his art to represent the exigency of that choice. If the remaking of style by the artist in order to represent a new view of life which has superseded the old is a heroic endeavor, it is one in which Hopkins—as we compare the first "St. Dorothea" and the ecstatic "Pied Beauty" with the tortured "Spelt from Sibyl's Leaves"—

succeeded. And if the ethical responsibility of a poet lies in his achievement of emotional accuracy through his evolving imaginative, structural, and linguistic mimesis, then Hopkins is, as he would have hoped, supremely ethical in each of his stages. We have seen the young poet of the second "St. Dorothea" timidly beginning to register a mild sensuous instress in a trochaic and spondaic rhythm; we have beheld the priest of "The Deutschland" inventing a prosody to embody the double rhythm of assaultive and relenting sensuousness as he inscapes and instresses the world; we know his delighted response to the natural world in "Pied Beauty" and "Moonrise," the one quickened and even threatened with opposites, the other guiltlessly lulling its tension into trance; but we also know—from "To what serves Mortal Beauty?"—the moral agitation about the dangerous world of sexual response to male beauty that creates a poetic structure which darts in zigzags from sensual glance to theology or thinking and back again in order to preserve a "just," or ethically responsible, aesthetic moment. We know, finally, the effort to restore Christ's likeness in man through arduous chromatic and asymptotic synonymy as it culminates in the supreme prophetic aesthetic tautology of crystalline redemption; and we know, equally well, the dissolution of the aesthetic moment into the starkly ethical one, accompanied by the grinding fear that that redemption will be lost at the moment of final eschatological choice. When the mind becomes one gigantic cacophony of groans, in eight-beat sprung-rhythm lines prolonging themselves into one undifferentiated monosyllabic vocal disharmony, we have come to the last agony of the stylistic body of poetry. Without Hopkins' remaking of the body of style, we would not come to know any of these things with that mimetic accuracy—one not only of visual representation but of structural and rhythmic enactment—which is the virtue, the fundamental ethics, of art.

Seamus Heaney:
The Grammatical Moment

• • •

Seamus Heaney's style—in the fullest sense of that word—has changed several times while retaining something "Heaneyesque" throughout. It would be easy to describe large changes in style marking Heaney's career—as rural idylls, for instance, gave way to social testaments in the years between *Death of a Naturalist* and *North*—but those changes have been much noticed. I want to address, rather, the way Heaney's style changes from poem to poem. I will be going backward from the present, chiefly because I have been deeply struck by the apparent bareness and simplicity of some recent poems in *Seeing Things* (1991). When I was looking into that bareness, I realized that in some instances it sprang from a poem's concentration on a single grammatical element. This gave me the springboard I needed to investigate how Heaney changes his style from poem to poem; and so I want to take up, in turn, four different "parts of speech" (as they used to be called) which have generated, in Heaney, different sorts of poems.

The first is the noun (in which I include the nominal phrase), and my example of a noun-poem is Poem xxiv from the forty-eight-poem, four-part sequence "Squarings" found in *Seeing Things*. The sequence is called "Squarings" because each of its poems looks like a square (each has five beats across and twelve lines down, a form "squarer" than the rectangular pentameter sonnet of fourteen lines). A square poem can resist the built-in binarism of the sonnet, which so often splits into question and answer, problem and solution. Poem xxiv is taken from the subsection of "Squarings" called "Settings"—a word implying life's backdrops, scenes which remain static while various dynamisms take place in front of or within them. The theory of "Settings" is announced in Poem xix:

> Memory as a building or a city,
> Well-lighted, well laid out, appointed with
> *Tableaux vivants* and costumed effigies.

According to Renaissance mnemonic theory, memories should be placed in mentally visualized settings so that the mind's eye can learn to recall its own contents in meaningful order:

> Ancient textbooks recommended that
>
> Familiar places be linked deliberately
> With a code of images. You knew the portent
> In each setting, you blinked and concentrated.
> (*Seeing Things,* 73)

"You knew the portent in each setting." The command behind Heaney's poems of settings is an epistemological one: *know.* One knows first a phenomenology perceived through the senses, a "setting." But that does not complete knowledge: one must also know the *portent.* This portent is not known through a deduction which succeeds phenomenological perception. Nor is the portent known emblematically, *through* the setting, but sensuously, *in* the setting. The task Heaney has set himself is not one of allegory but one of what we might call clairvoyant perception. The settings are symbolic not of something beyond themselves but of something *in* themselves. A setting is something now re-seen, in the retrospect of middle age, *as* portending at the time it was experienced, even if one did not, in the past moment, recognize the portent in the setting.

How does this theory of a mnemonic possession of past portent enact itself in style? "In a poetry of the noun," is the short answer. Verbs, under the sway of this poetics, become nouns themselves (gerunds), or they attach themselves, as past-participle adjectives, to nouns. Instead of "genuine" or well-formed narrative sentences, exhibiting their unavoidable temporality in the verb, we find sentences composed almost exclusively of nouns or noun-phrases:

Deserted harbour stillness. Every stone
Clarified and dormant under water,
The harbour wall a masonry of silence.

Fullness. Shimmer. Laden high Atlantic
The moorings barely stirred in, very slight
Clucking of the swell against boat boards.

Perfected vision: cockle minarets
Consigned down there with green-slicked bottle
    glass,
Shell-debris and a reddened bud of sandstone.

Air and ocean known as antecedents
Of each other. In apposition with
Omnipresence, equilibrium, brim.

(78)

The word "known" rules over the last tercet here as it did over the last tercet of the earlier "theory" sonnet, Poem xix. Words resembling "to know" inhabit other poems within the "Settings" group: "to watch," "to witness," "to sense," "to rediscover," "to see," "to feel," "to remember," and "to imagine." Such words suggest that these "squarings" are poems recollected in tranquillity. But they have changed Wordsworth's emphasis: unlike Heaney, Wordsworth, in such memory-poems, often actively reenters and reenacts the past episode. Of the daffodils, he says,

> For oft, when on my couch I lie,
> In vacant or in pensive mood,
> They flash upon that inward eye
> Which is the bliss of solitude;
> And then *my heart with pleasure fills,*
> *And dances with the daffodils.*
>   ("I Wandered Lonely As a Cloud")

Like Heaney, however, Wordsworth sometimes shows recollected experience to be of unknown portent:

>   I made no vows, but vows
> Were then made for me; *bond unknown to me*
> *Was given,* that I should be, else sinning greatly,
> A dedicated Spirit.
>   (*The Prelude*, IV, 341–344)

Like Wordsworth's dawn memory in *The Prelude*, Heaney's portents were unconsciously stored away in childhood, youth, and the more recent past; they were not seen at the time as portents of what the poet would become. It is only now, recalling the scenes that were mysteriously stored away (in implicit contrast with other, forgotten scenes) that Heaney can ask why these, precisely, were the deeply engraved scenes of portent. He calls them up in verse, this time to raise into consciousness the portent within them. This second, poetic, representation takes place as if in the static trance of second sight: the senses register sight, sound, movement, relation, but the observer is forbidden to intervene. Through the scrim of memory there can be no penetration by present agency, no dancing with past daffodils. Since the most static part of speech is the noun, nouns must be the part of speech to govern the style of a poem written under such a poetics of trance. Yet not any sort of noun will do; for interpretation, we must look at the species of noun as well.

The nouns in Poem xxiv are *stillness, stone, water, wall, masonry, silence, fullness, shimmer, Atlantic, moorings, clucking, swell, boards, vision, minarets, glass, debris, bud, sandstone, air, ocean, antecedents, apposition, omnipresence, equilibrium,* and *brim.* These nouns can be divided into four subsets or species. The first (unproblematic) subset is one of common nouns representing "real things," and these are *harbour, stone, wall, moorings, swell, boards, glass, debris, sandstone, air,* and *ocean.* These "things" compose the first level of the setting. The second subset of nouns, slightly more airy but still visibly drawn from "the real," is one of "real things" metaphorically applied, as *masonry* becomes a figure for silence, *clucking* becomes a figure for the ocean's sound, *minarets* a figure for cockles, and *bud* a figure for a small red stone.

The third subset of nouns is one of "reified adjectives" and "reified verbs": the adjectives *still, silent, full, omnipresent* here become *stillness, silence, fullness,* and *omnipresence;* the verbs *shimmer* and *brim* are here used as nouns. The qualities that would in "real life" have been represented by adjectives ("silent") or verbs ("brim") are here put under the still sign of noun-trance. A famous earlier poem in a similar setting does its adjectives "straight":

> The sea is *calm* tonight,
> The tide is *full,* the moon lies *fair*
> Upon the straits; . . .
>> the cliffs of England stand,
> *Glimmering* and *vast,* out in the *tranquil* bay.
>> (Matthew Arnold, "Dover Beach")

A Heaney-trance would transform this into: *calmness; fullness; fairness; glimmer; vastness; tranquillity.* Such a move would put us into the realm of *x-ness,* of suspension in quality, where nothing can happen. This realm of *x-ness* completes its nominal phrases with past participles representing finishedness: all is *deserted, clarified, laden, perfected, consigned, known.* Just as action is not possible in suspendedness, so it is not possible in finishedness. (Motion in Heaney's poem comes only from the Atlantic swell, making—in a dependent adjective clause—the moorings stir, clucking against the hulls of boats.)

The fourth subset of nouns in the poem is one of relationship: *antecedents, apposition, equilibrium.* Their Latin prefixes (*ante-, ad-,* and *equi-*) incorporate beforeness, withness, and balancedness, each a condition requiring two things. These nouns offer us two ways of viewing the trance in which memory is revived as portent. The trance is, first of all, paradoxical (since two things cannot both be antecedents to each other). The trance is also one of simultaneity, as the "real" (air and ocean) can be seen in apposition with any one of three subsequent things: the metaphysical (which brings forward a theological word like "omnipresence"); the cognitive (which brings forward a scientific word like "equilibrium"); or the kinesthetic (which brings forward a physically felt word like "brim").

It is no accident that two of the relational nouns—"antecedent" and "apposition"—are terms drawn from grammar, because the trance of "the portent recognized" can be expressed only in a written grammar posterior to experience. As a pronoun refers to its antecedent, so the portent recognized refers to an originating experience. But as it is the later recognition of portent that sends one back to the past for confirmation, the recognition is also the antecedent, cognitively speaking, of the recovered phenomenon. Experience is the necessary antecedent of written recognition; but re-cognition in language is the antecedent by which the portent is revealed to have been implicit all the while in originary experience. Apposition, on the other hand, unlike antecedence, is not a temporal figure. Once antecedence is postulated of both sides, of both life *and* writing, that paradoxical reciprocity can repose in the richness for which apposition is the rhetorical figure—the

figure of pressed-down and running-over, the figure of brimful-
ness, balance, the blissful undifferentiation of omnipresence.

Such is the pressure of nounness on this poem that even its
adjectives are mostly nouns: "*harbour* stillness," "*harbour* wall,"
"*boat* boards," "*cockle* minarets," "*bottle* glass," "*shell*-debris."
What does this figure—the presence of persistently nominal ad-
jectives—stand for in Heaney's memorial trance? It stands of
course for incorporation, since this figure is either one of conden-
sation of a possessive phrase—"the stillness of the harbour," "the
boards of the boat"—or one of superposition, as cockles which
resemble minarets become "cockle-minarets." Things which are
conceptually kept on different levels (a "harbour" and "stillness")
become mutually implicated, filtered through the single moment
of their recurrence as imaginative portent.

But of what is this scene a "portent"? It is necessary here to
recall a very different set of scenes—the many childhood scenes
in Heaney's volumes which point up a binary contrast. For in-
stance, one could think of Heaney's poem "The Other Side," in
which a Protestant neighbor visits the Heaneys' Catholic farm.
These binary experiences are summed up in Heaney's poem "Ter-
minus," which analyzes his own necessarily binary responses—"Is
it any wonder that when I thought / I would have second
thoughts?" (*Selected Poems*, 234). The many anxieties that break
through and distract Heaney's moments of repose—anxieties epito-
mized by the rat on the briar in "Glanmore Revisited"—are so
constant that they seem intrinsic to his art and unavoidable. Yet
the trance-poem I have been looking at tells us that the cohesive
and integrative feeling of "Omnipresence, equilibrium, brim" has
become available to Heaney in later life, and that the portent of
this relatively late psychic state of wholeness can be located in the
perceptual rapture that Heaney felt in one earlier day of "per-
fected vision" in a deserted harbor. The harbor moment was a
portent of a time when his vision would not necessarily be binary,
his thoughts not always second thoughts.

Can every adult emotional and cognitive state, even a late one, find its earlier perceptual portent? And if so, how is that connection between then and now apprehended? The harbor poem suggests that a certain sort of reanimation of the past—not reliving the perceptual experience as it was encountered, as Wordsworth did with the daffodils, but rather reconstructing it transfixed but projected forward—is a way to create a third realm, neither one of pure memory actively revived nor one of present distanced actuality, but rather one of the past remembered forward as prophecy. The past is now necessarily conceptualized and therefore kinetically immobile; it is sensed in nouns of almost paradisal balance—mutual *antecedents, apposition, omnipresence, equilibrium, brim.*

How can this writer of nouns be the Heaney who, in "Oysters," the marvelous opening poem of *Field Work* (1979), vowed to be "verb, all verb"? "Oysters" itself wants to be all verb, and it begins with an opening arc of verbs and verbs-turned-adjectives which connect the mundane oysters, their consumer the poet, and the lofty constellations themselves:

> Our shells *clacked* on the plates.
> My tongue was a *filling* estuary,
> My palate *hung* with starlight.
> As I *tasted* the salty Pleiades
> Orion *dipped* his foot into the water.

And the very stanzas of "Oysters" are organized by verbs—the oysters *lay*, we *had driven,* the Romans *hauled,* I *ate* the day. Yet, for all his energetic verbs, the speaker spoils his innocent appetite with misery and second thoughts. His own sexual and political anxieties keep him from resting in the material happiness of the day; they make him align the oysters he is eating both with victimized women, "alive and violated," and with the imported oysters that the richer Romans had expensively hauled to Rome for their delectation—"the frond-lipped, brine-stung / Glut of privilege":

> [I] was angry that my trust could not repose
> In the clear light, like poetry or freedom,
> Leaning in from sea. I ate the day
> Deliberately, that its tang
> Might quicken me all into verb, pure verb.
>
> (*Selected Poems*, 107)

"Verb," then, for Heaney, stands for an immediate sensual apprehension of life unspoiled by sexual or political second thoughts. Yet the ambition to be "verb, pure verb" is not often fulfilled in *Field Work*, haunted as it is by guilty meditation on "the murdered dead" ("The Badgers"). A softer version of the wish to be "verb, pure verb" appears in the painful close of "The Guttural Muse," where Heaney abandons the hope of being a public healer in favor of the less ambitious wish to regain inner feeling:

> I felt like some old pike all badged with sores
> Wanting to swim in touch with soft-mouthed life.
>
> (*Selected Poems*, 123)

The impotent verb here—"wanting to swim"—cannot connect actively with that erotic "life" that the poet sees happening below his hotel window.

Where, then, are the lost action-verbs? They are most unselfconsciously present in Heaney's poems of childhood, where they arise as if by themselves, as they do when the boy, with his mother, folds sheets fresh off the line:

> . . . I *took* my corners of the linen
> And *pulled* against her, first straight down the hem

And then diagonally, then *flapped* and *shook*
The fabric like a sail in a cross wind.

(250)

But can such actions—unthinking, habitual, familial—sustain adult life? The longing for "pure verb" appears in *Field Work* chiefly as frustration. The poet can see, watch, and endure: he can wait in retirement in Glanmore and see active ghosts "come striding into their spring stations" (*Selected Poems*, 124), but he himself can only dream of "break[ing] through," "Sudden and sure as the man who dared the ice / And raced his bike across the Moyola River" (129). The poet himself does not race: "We toe the line / between the tree in leaf and the bare tree" ("September Song"; *Field Work*, 43). When *Field Work*, after its long puzzling over inactivity, finds its adult active verbs at last, it is during an incident between the poet and his wife. The currant bush at Glanmore has opened its pink blooms with their unexpectedly acrid "catspiss smell." Seeing the blossoming bush, the poet breaks into the most primitive art-action conceivable, using a succession of deliberate and willed verbs. First, he primes the skin of his wife's hand with a leaf-shape from leaf-juice:

I press a leaf
of the flowering currant
on the back of your hand
for the tight slow burn
of its sticky juice
to prime your skin,
and your veins to be crossed
criss-cross with leaf veins.

The chiasmus *veins* : *crossed* :: *cross* : *veins* enacts the priming as magic ritual. Next, the speaker, in a succession of active verbs, coats the sticky primed skin-canvas with a layer of painted-on earth:

I lick my thumb
and dip it in mould,
I anoint the anointed
leaf-shape. Mould
blooms and pigments
the back of your hand
like a birthmark—
my umber one,
you are stained, stained
to perfection.

   (*Selected Poems,* 140)

What is it that has liberated the hesitant poet, trapped in states of impotent watching, into "verb, pure verb"? It is the discovery that perfection is not immaculate but maculate. These verbs—"I lick . . . and dip, . . . I anoint"—are ritual sacramental verbs, vaguely baptismal, vaguely confirmational. The reclaiming of the maculate body—male and female—under the signs of sticky leaf-juice (life-juice) and adhering earth ("dust thou art") enables decisive action at last for one who has long seen himself as an indecisive and yearning observer, estranged from his first, famous verb-declaration about his pen (a substitute for his father's spade)—"I'll dig with it."

If the most recent Heaney is a poet of the noun, if the sensual Heaney is a poet of the verb, the earliest Heaney seemed, to me, a poet of the adjective. There were of course narratives in the early verse, as the boy of the poems was frightened by croaking frogs or disappointed by his blackberries rotting overnight, but the story lines were less memorable than the adjectives and adjectival phrases that festooned them. The "green and heavy-headed" flax, the "warm thick slobber of frogspawn," the "clotted" water, the "gross-bellied" frogs with their "loose necks," the "blunt heads" on the "great slime kings"—to quote only a few rich and luscious adjectives from "Death of a Naturalist" (*Selected Poems,* 5–6)— made the turbid natural world bubble and ooze from Heaney's page. Sensuous and tactile, such adjectives were as useful for wells and windlasses as for thatch and butterpats. The conviction that the adjectival is inexhaustible, that the process of definition by description is endless, lies behind the early *ars poetica* voiced in "Bogland":

> The ground itself is kind, black butter
>
> Melting and opening underfoot,
> Missing its last definition
> By millions of years. . . .
>
> The wet centre is bottomless.
>
> (22–23)

As I have said, Heaney was from his youth naturally adjectival in a Keatsian way. But what does it mean to Heaney, at the height of his powers in *North*, to write in deliberate adjectives? The endpoint of the adjectival is of course the analogical, expressed by simile and metaphor. And it is to such endpoints that Heaney is driving as he conducts his battle, by means of the adjectival, against the denotative in language. Heaney's masterpiece in *North*, "The Grauballe Man" (*Selected Poems*, 82–83), amounts to a defense of poetry as it resorts, against the flatness of the denotative noun, to the adjectival sublime, which incites the imagination to its utmost stretch.

In "The Grauballe Man," Heaney sees a murdered body that has been tanned by earth acids during its long burial in a Jutland bog. Disinterred, the body challenges, even defies, description. The ordinary denotative words for this spectacle are the flat nouns "corpse" and "body," but the poet indignantly rejects them as inadequate:

> Who will say 'corpse'
> to his vivid cast?

Who will say 'body'
to his opaque repose?

The poet has made the preserved body of the Grauballe Man a
site of contrast between our normal denotative nouns—"corpse"
and "body"—and his own adjectivally modified abstract nouns—
"cast" and "repose." The adjectives "vivid" and "opaque" are
mutually contradictory, as are the two abstract nouns: "cast" turns
the corpse into a bronze statue, while "repose" turns it into a
sleeping man. It is against those who would carelessly say "corpse"
or "body" that the poem erects its simulacrum-in-language of the
Grauballe Man. Each of its adjectival descriptions is another cast-
ing of the corpse in the bronze of art, each of its analogies another
command resurrecting the body from its "opaque repose."

For it is nothing other than resurrection that is at issue in
Heaney's adjectival power. Can the poet transform the Grauballe
Man—that "corpse," that "body" (in the inattentive world's eyes)—
into a "vivid cast" of art or a living body stretched out in strange
repose? The poet's use of the word "opaque" tells us that he
himself is not yet certain what is betokened in and by that repose;
it will be by adjectival suppositions, imaginative casts made one
after the other, that the beholder may discover what is obscured
by that opacity. The adjectival suppositions must be true to the
eerily unearthed figure lying before the beholder, a figure seen
first in a photograph, secondly in a museum, and thirdly in mem-
ory; but they must hint, too, at the prehistory of the figure, before
it became what the callous world would demean with the words
"corpse" and "body."

The poet's first adjectival suppositions, introduced by the words
"as if" and "seems," offer a view of the whole Grauballe Man:

As if he had been poured
in tar, he lies

on a pillow of turf
and seems to weep

the black river of himself.

The initial supposition makes the man the result of a liquid
process like the casting of molten bronze; but because of the
figure's black surface, the poet conjectures that this strangely
beautiful statue was "poured in tar." Through the second suppo-
sition, the effigy is transmuted into a person in repose: "he lies /
on a pillow." In the third supposition, the statue/person is given
agency and self-originating metamorphic Ovidian power in the
present: he "seems to weep / the black river of himself." The
"black river" is a phrase redolent of Styx and Lethe; as a river
lying between the gazing spectator and the unknown origin of
his victimage, the Grauballe Man takes on a geographic, natural,
and heroic grandeur larger than that proper even to his existence
as a statue or to his being as a person.

As the poem passes from a view of the whole man to a view of
his anatomical parts, the adjectival suppositions resort to the
words "like" and "as," continuing the poet's self-reflexive sense
(already visible in his "as if" and "seems") of a conscious search
for analogues. "Like" and "as" mark the new analogues rhetori-
cally as simile:

The grain of his wrists
is like bog oak,
the ball of his heel

like a basalt egg.
His instep has shrunk
cold as a swan's foot
or a wet swamp root.

In the poet's first search for the proper adjectival predication, the
similes tend toward the inanimate—bog oak, a basalt egg, a swamp

root. But the penultimate animate but dissociated bird-part—the cold swan's foot—heralds the animate metaphors to follow.

Probe after probe enters the reclining figure's unknown substance: Is he stone? Is he tough bird-tissue? Is he a gnarled root? The probes are successively visual and tactile, and are sometimes two-dimensional ("the grain of his wrists"), sometimes three-dimensional ("the ball of his heel"). The corpse, at this point, is still unresurrected: it is stony, wooden, cold, alien, made of disarticulated parts. But as the similes turn to metaphors, the corpse begins to stir. Although its parts are still disarticulated, the metaphors used to describe them are integral creatures, creatures who are alive and move:

> His hips are the ridge
> and purse of a mussel,
> his spine an eel arrested
> under a glisten of mud.

And then there arrive the startling and revelatory moments of animation: "The head lifts," followed by "The . . . wound / opens." There is no longer any "as if" or "seems" or "like" or "as." The gradual penetration of the poet into the Grauballe Man's opacity has been rewarded by a clarity of perception, by means of which the poet sees into the darkest depths of the body:

> The head lifts,
> the chin is a visor
> raised above the vent
> of his slashed throat
>
> that has tanned and toughened.
> The cured wound
> opens inwards to a dark
> elderberry place.

Here, the metaphorical suppositions ("visor," "toughened," "cured") give human character to what had previously been part inorganic, part organic, part animal—a basalt egg, a swamp root, an arrested eel. Now, this creature wears a warrior's visor—even if that visor is only his backward-forced chin, displaced by the knife-slash that killed him. And the creature is given an implied moral character; his throat has "tanned and toughened." His wound, in a grave pun, is both "cured," as by tanning, and "cured," as by healing. But the last adjectival supposition of the inventory is the most daring of all. "Inside this disturbing darkness of surface lies what darkness of decay?" asks the investigating and probing mind. Instead of decay, however, it finds, at the pit of the ancient wound, regenerative fruit—an "elderberry place." The Tollund Man was found with "his last gruel of winter seeds / Caked in his stomach" (*Selected Poems,* 39), and Heaney's Bog Queen tells us that in her long underground burial, her brain, darkening, was "a jar of spawn / fermenting underground" (79). These inner darknesses are reproductive, like the barley in the pockets of the buried Croppies, sprouting the next August after their death ("Requiem for the Croppies").

It is only after the "miraculous" independent resurrective motions of the lifting head and the opening wound, themselves brought about by Heaney's successive adjectival casts, that the poet defends his own perception of the Grauballe Man, saying that the figure is inadequately described by the denotative nouns "corpse" and "body." Having raised the victim from the dead, having seen him with his slashed throat gaping in reproach, Heaney feels tenderness awaken in himself. He cannot leave his mummified Jutland figure in this plight, any more than Jesus would have done with Lazarus. The *disjecta membra* must be rearticulated, the victim given a pre-slaughter innocence. Similes now return as the poet recalls his first sight, in a photograph in P. V. Glob's book *The Bog People,* of the Grauballe Man; the corpse is now reversed in time to become a newborn baby, though with the mark of antiquity upon him through the word "rusted":

And his rusted hair,
a mat unlikely
as a foetus's.
I first saw his twisted face

in a photograph,
a head and shoulder
out of the peat,
bruised like a forceps baby.

But the restored innocence of a fetus or a newborn baby is not sufficient: the Grauballe Man must be restored to dignity as well. As the poem moves into the moment ("now") of its own composition, the poet's two anterior experiences—the initial sight of the Grauballe Man in the photograph and the subsequent sight of the actual body in Jutland—move into the past realm of perfected memory:

but now he lies
perfected in my memory
down to the red horn
of his nails.

"The red horn of his nails" returns us to metaphor once again, after the more detached similes of the fetus and the baby. The nails, after their underground tanning and curing, have come to resemble horn—a material, like nails, intermediate between the inert and the alive, and a material (like bog oak, basalt, and root-wood) suitable for the hand of the sculptor. The imagination is ready for its last adjectival hypothesis, as it balances, against the beauty of the "cast" Grauballe Man as sculpture, the atrocity of his human death. The figure, now recollected, is suspended,

hung in the scales
with beauty and atrocity.

On the left, the Grauballe Man is placed with any beauty made out of violence,

> with the Dying Gaul
> too strictly compassed
>
> on his shield.

On the right, the Grauballe Man is placed with social atrocity uninterpreted by art:

> with the actual weight
> of each hooded victim
> slashed and dumped.

As Heaney said in 1974 of the bog bodies, "The unforgettable photographs of these victims blended in my mind with photographs of atrocity, past and present, in the long rites of Irish political and religious struggles" (*Preoccupations*, 57–58).

If we stand back from these repeated casts of the imagination into the descriptive mode, as it searches for similes and metaphors adequate to its daunting prehistoric object, we can see that, grammatically speaking, the poem employs a generous supply of verbs ("he seems to weep") and nouns ("a basalt egg") as well as adjectives. But the *effort* of all the phrases is ultimately adjectival: What can be invented by way of description that will render this figure something other than "corpse" or "body"? The ultimate effect of the Heaney adjectival effort is of course "pure verb"— the corpse lifts its head, is reanimated, and is even reborn. But in "perfected memory," the Grauballe Man is once again inert, in two ways: as artwork, yes, insofar as he is compassed in Heaney's poem as the Dying Gaul was aesthetically compassed on his shield. The artist's own critique of his art is that the Grauballe Man's kinetic potential is greater than the poem's descriptive compass— which is too strict for its content—just as the disposition of the body of the Dying Gaul, in the Celtic bronze of that name, coerces the figure (in order to put it into a stylized relation to the round shield) into something other than the natural posture of a fallen soldier. The "too strict" aestheticized construction of the body therefore cannot be used to close the poem, but yields to the second "perfected" inertia, that of the victim shrouded in the past participles of alien agency, menacingly "slashed" and "dumped." These are the last adjectival casts of the poet, his last look at the Grauballe Man, and they are relentlessly "unpoetic."

The nature of adjectival poems is to be radial. All of Heaney's hazarding adjectival casts, radiating out from a central baffling subject, are the means of seeing by facets a subject too imaginatively overwhelming to be grasped as a whole. They are a way of encompassing perplexity, of encouraging the opaque into transparency. But Heaney is too greatly disturbed by, and exalted by, the Grauballe Man to employ solely the radial structure natural to the adjectival mode. He consequently welds the radial structure to an ongoing linear investigation of itself by "baring the device" (as the Russian Formalists would have said), moving linearly from his "as if" and "seems" through "like" and "as" to metaphor itself in its divine and resurrective aliveness: "the head lifts." The poem then proceeds to unravel its own miracle, returning to "as" and "like" as it reverses the corpse to babyhood. Finally, the poem formally enacts its own dilemma of adjectival description: it conjures up the beauty of art and the atrocity of violence as two opposing pan-weights of a single scale. The forked ending suggests that adjectival art-description, though it may bring about both elucidation of essence and a temporary reanimation of sorts, cannot, in its strict compass, match the kinetic potential of life. Adjectival endeavor ends either with a consent to stylization (the Gaul on his shield) or with a recognition of the irremediable unstylizability of the mortal, always slashed and dumped beyond either religious or aesthetic resurrection.

In speaking of parts of speech—nouns, verbs, adjectives—as

indicators of changes of style in Heaney, I do not mean to slight
other equally powerful indices of style such as imagery and genre.
But these latter are easier to see, since they are the vehicles for
well-known macrostories—that of the rural poet turned political,
or that of the sonneteer of Glanmore turned revenant on Station
Island. The macrostories of content are already familiar, the mi-
crostories of style less so.

I want to end with another, less noticed part of speech, the
adverb. Often, when I feel that a given poem by Heaney sounds
different from one I read not long before, I can put my finger on
the difference in style—which to me means a different deploy-
ment of life and attitude—only by looking at the grammatical
structure of the poem. So it is with one of Heaney's most dazzling
and succinct poems of self-definition, a 1984 poem I have already
mentioned called "Terminus" (*Selected Poems*, 234–235):

Terminus

I

When I hoked there, I would find
An acorn and a rusted bolt.

If I lifted my eyes, a factory chimney
And a dormant mountain.

If I listened, an engine shunting
And a trotting horse.

Is it any wonder when I thought
I would have second thoughts?

II

When they spoke of the prudent squirrel's hoard
It shone like gifts at a nativity.

When they spoke of the mammon of iniquity
The coins in my pockets reddened like stove-lids.

I was the march drain and the march drain's banks
Suffering the limit of each claim.

III

Two buckets were easier carried than one.
I grew up in between.

My left hand placed the standard iron weight.
My right tilted a last grain in the balance.

Baronies, parishes met where I was born.
When I stood on the central stepping stone

I was the last earl on horseback in midstream
Still parleying, in earshot of his peers.

"Terminus" asks that we think about two categories of self-definition. The first is a temporally incremental one represented here by adverbial clauses of action, "When I" or "If I." The second is a more static and spatial self-definition, one represented in the poem by the simple adverb "in between," and by various images: a stream (the "march drain") marking the border of adjoining "marches"; two balanced yoked buckets; a balance-scale; demarcations between two parishes; and an earl on horseback in midstream, halted, parleying with his enemies. Heaney's long chain of adverbial clauses composes the framing grammatical armature of the poem, from the opening "When I hoked there" to the closing "When I stood." The "When I"'s of the young boy in Parts I and III bracket the "When they"'s of his parents in Part II.

A poem so frontally and continually adverbial draws us into the heart of what the adverbial means, what we use it for. Here, its function is to construct simultaneity. As we have seen, in Heaney's "perfected vision," air and ocean are antecedents of each other, each reciprocally constituting the other in the simultaneity of perception. So, in "Terminus," self-formation is a process by which two aspects of the psyche are formed at once reciprocally. The adverbial phrases in "Terminus" are habitual ones, in which "when" and "if" come close to meaning "whenever" and "often if." Here is the adverbial scheme of simultaneity, reduced:

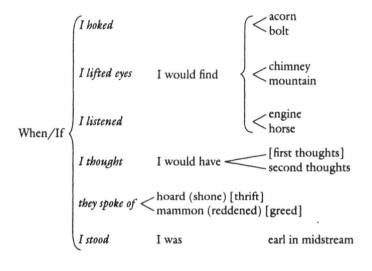

Such a poem, beginning and ending in the march drain which serves as Heaney's startling self-image in Part II, enacts self-formation as a constant dialogue, through act and sensation, with one's environment. Whereas Wordsworth presents an exclusively rural scene that fosters the child by successive ministries of beauty and fear, Heaney lets us glimpse a set of surroundings both industrial and rural, where a retrieved machine-made bolt coincides with a retrieved acorn, where a factory chimney is silhouetted against a mountain, and where the noise of an engine is heard, stereoscopically, at the same time as the trotting of a horse. (The latter two are troublingly similar: "an engine shunting" and "a trotting horse" give the iron horse a gait-exercise as natural to it as trotting is to its flesh-and-blood brother.) Heaney's adverbial clauses remind us that sight is not a *result* of seeing, nor sound a *result* of hearing; rather, "seeing" is seeing *something*, "hearing" is hearing *something*. "Hoking" is hoking *something*, too, since the very meaning of the dialect word "hoking" is "to pull something up with a hooked probing-tool." In this way, we are made to see, by adverbiality, that the child has no choice—in pure simultaneity, his hoking is dual, his scenery is binary, his hearing is stereophonic. Though the physical simultaneity of "hearing" and "hearing something" is perfectly reflected by the syntax of the adverbial modifiers "when" and "if," there remains nonetheless a conceptual (and verbal) distinction between the sensation and its object—"If I listened, [I would find] an engine . . . / And a horse." Perfect simultaneity of both syntax and content is enacted only in the metaphysical adverbial moment in which thought thinks itself: "When I *thought* / I would have second *thoughts*."

In "Terminus," Heaney is explaining his own intelligence to himself. It is perplexing to see one's fellow citizens, like oneself in so many ways, taking on passionate ideological positions of the left or the right. It is not only the repellent content of one-dimensional ideological positions that is in question here; it is the intrinsic repellency of intransigent position-taking itself. In any moment in which there is right on both sides (and this is the usual human case), ideological intransigence stands in direct conflict with both imaginative sympathy and moral complexity. (Heaney is concerned here not with position-taking on absolute evil, but rather with position-taking on such conflicts as rural preservation versus industrial modernization.) Other such conflicts that are mentioned in the poem include the morality of saving money (is it the commendable thrift of the squirrel or the depravity of mammon?), the resolution of border disputes, contractual dealing, and military conflict. Convincing human arguments can generally be mounted on both sides of such questions; but ideologues have *a priori* positions that do not admit dialogue. Rebuked by ideologues as a Mr. Facing-Both-Ways, and wondering why he tends to respond with an incurably dual view of conflict, Heaney, only partly in whimsy, here recalls his early dual imprinting by sight and sound and even by the diversion of "hoking." Equally, one's childhood confusion, he suggests, can stem from the conceptual conflict of various parentally endorsed moral parables, setting the Aesopian prudence of the squirrel in one against the biblical prohibition of hoarding the mammon of iniquity in another.

So far, in dwelling on the way that adverbial clauses enact the paradoxical simultaneity of antithetical stimuli, I have neglected to return to Heaney's internal rupture of his opening and closing adverbial frame by central nonadverbially modified first-person declarative sentences—"I was the march drain . . . I grew up. . . . / My left hand placed . . . / My right tilted a last grain." This declarative rupture of the adverbial produces one of those grammatical shocks to which Heaney so naturally resorts. The *temporal* simultaneity of hoking the hoked, of seeing the seen, hearing the heard, and thinking thoughts is replaced, in the center of "Terminus," by the *spatial* simultaneity of being at once a stream dividing two parishes and the banks of that stream, as the stream suffers simultaneously "the limits of each claim." "From the beginning," Heaney said in a 1985 conversation with Neil Corcoran, "I was very conscious of boundaries":

> There was a drain or stream, the Sluggan drain, an old division that ran very close to our house. It divided the townland of Tamniarn from the townland of Anahorish and those two townlands belonged in two different parishes, Bellaghy and Newbridge, which are also in two different dioceses: the diocese of Derry ended at the Sluggan drain and the diocese of Armagh began. I was always going backward and forwards. . . . I seemed always to be a little displaced; being in between was a kind of condition, from the start. (Corcoran, *Seamus Heaney,* 13)

The indices of simultaneity in the spatial couplet concerning the march drain are the "and" joining drain and banks, and the "-ing" of the continuous suffering of the stream as it feels pressure from both banks, a pressure experienced as the "limit" of each claim. The stream tries to expand to the left, and is limited by the leftist claim; it tries to expand to the right, and is limited by the rightist claim. The experience of ideological claims as limits, rather than as solaces or solicitings (as their partisans might describe them) is a response that Heaney is still endeavoring to explain to himself, because the banks are also himself. He is not simply the fluid stream, balked and checked by the unwelcome rigidities of the earth; he is also the home soil anxiously checking, from both left and right, his own perhaps (as he worries) too flexible current.

The resort to a spatial image in its center carries the poem away from temporal simultaneity. The model in the center is not "When this, that." It is "Both this *and* that," both drain *and* banks, both bucket A *and* bucket B. Why? Because "Two buckets were easier carried than one," a pragmatic answer arrived at after the experiment of hauling one bucket alone. This is not the necessitarian seeing of sights or thinking of thoughts. The child who was once passive under stimuli of sight or hearing is now active, and choosing. In the next image of both/and, he is a human scale, with his left hand serving as the left pan with a standard weight (civil convention) in it, his right hand a pan containing a contractual measure of grain. This is the emblematic scale of justice where equivalence is fairly determined between elements different in kind. Nature (the grain) and social convention (the standard weight) here find their simultaneity in the human scale of justice. The last spatial simultaneity of both/and allows for the youth's recognition of the presence of contending powers, sacred and profane—church parishes and feudal baronies—as "Render unto God" coexists with "Render unto Caesar."

If the poem had stopped here, the central "both/and" model

of spiritual/secular dualism would have replaced the initial "when/then" model of adverbial simultaneity; and we would have seen the earlier "when/then" as a model for childhood perceptual passivity and the second "both/and" as a model for a more adult pragmatic and ethical choice, one which enacts civil justice and is aware of secular and spiritual distinctions. This hypothesis, however, would not explain the reversion of the poem (as it makes its concluding statement) to the initial "when/then" model we have so far associated with childhood:

When I stood on the central stepping stone

I was the last earl on horseback in midstream
Still parleying, in earshot of his peers.

This "when/then" statement—the only one enjambed over a stanza break—brings into simultaneity not a function and its object (seeing a sight) nor elder speech and its effect on the child (as when money—depending on which was the more recent authoritative parental phrase—shone like Babylonian gold or reddened like demonic fire), but rather it brings into simultaneity the child's independent action in venturing out to the stream's central stepping-stone and his equally independent act of historical fantasy. This act of imagination transforms him into a seventeenth-century Irish earl, unwilling to flee with his peers, still willing to negotiate with the enemy.*

Heaney's historical revisionism presents not the "Flight of the

---

*In 1607, as a coda to his 1601 defeat by the English at Kinsale, the last Gaelic Earl, Hugh O'Neil, second Earl of Tyrone, who had successfully "parleyed" for his autonomy with Lord Mountjoy under the reign of both Elizabeth and James, decided (in Roy Foster's terms) to "cut his losses, leaving Ireland with Rory O'Donnell, first Earl of Tyrconnell." "The Flight of the Earls" was much mythologized in Irish history as the definitive symbol of the collapse of Gaelic Ireland. See Roy Foster, *Modern Ireland, 1600–1972* (London: Penguin, 1988), 44.

Earls" as it is usually conceived—as the last Gaelic Earls abandon further relations with England and pack themselves off to the Continent—but as his own double-mindedness would rewrite the scene: himself in midstream, himself *the* midstream, still willing to parley with the invaders even as his peers—his fellow noblemen—are, we know, turning away from his negotiations and directing their horses toward the waiting ships. "Still parleying": *"Parle encore"* is the Muse's sole command to poets, even incipient ones. In historical fantasy, the boy-as-O'Neil still feels the limits of each claim—that of the English who, coopting him, made him an Earl and allowed him to keep his lands, but equally that of his decamping fellow Earls, deprived since the English conquest of real political sovereignty, to whom he is bound by language, religion, and custom. He parleys with the English while his peers—they are placed, by the poem, within earshot in this as yet undecided moment—may or may not listen to his parley. The decisive confluence here of midstream and parleying, in the last and conclusive adverbial simultaneity of the poem, suggests that the contemporary "parleying" of poetry—by contrast to the cant of *a priori* ideological position-taking—can arise only from one who has habitually been standing, since childhood, in mid-position between opposing perceptual and moral realities.

The styles I have been characterizing and examining—nominal, adjectival, verbal, and adverbial—represent only a sampling of Heaney's gift for conferring on different poems radically different grammatical textures, each of them enacting a coherent ensemble of feeling and thought. No other contemporary poet has so exquisite a sense of the cognitive and moral import of the parts of speech as they play their syntactic roles. This sense arises in part from Heaney's disciplined knowledge of three languages—English, Latin, Irish—in which grammatical and syntactic textures, sharpened by difference, make themselves distinctively felt. To move from one grammatical texture to another is a way of breaking one's style—less dramatic, no doubt, than Hopkins' aerobic leap into sprung rhythm, and less dramatic, too, than Heaney's own forcible burst into demotic language in "Whatever You Say, Say Nothing" and "Station Island." Yet for me the drama of going from the nominal to the adjectival, from the verbal to the adverbial, is thrillingly central to the perfecting of implication. A poem says a great deal by saying "I am written in verbs": it says, as "Field Work" (IV) does, "I have found at last an action in which I can believe, in which I can engage, which I can render sacramental, and which I can report as good." A poem written in adjectives, like "The Grauballe Man," says, "I am making successive casts to say what this phenomenon is like; I am hoping to revive it into verbal presence; I yearn to categorize it; I need to stylize it; can I succeed?" A poem written in adverbs says, "They happened together, these things: why? What is simultaneity? Is it a form of cause and effect, of necessity, of affective response, of practical reason, of imagination, of temperament, of fantasy? How is a lifelong simultaneity of perception connected to a revulsion from *a priori* judgment?" And finally (to return to the poem of harbor stillness), a poem written in nouns says, in the words of Faust to the transient moment, "Remain awhile, thou art so fair." Remain poised for twelve lines in the memorial squarings of language: say *omnipresence;* say *equilibrium;* say *brim.* The poem of nouns is a hymn to the ravishments of remembered sensation, a call to praise the portents of memory from the cockle-minarets of lyric.

It would be a mistake, perhaps, to end here on a lyric note. I should add that only an exceptional depth of lyric and linguistic self-consciousness in Heaney could lead to the exquisite stylizations of the poems I have taken up—and of many others of equal refinement of means. Heaney's poems have exhibited a remarkable power to move and impress readers with both private emotion and public anguish. It is not to detract from their large and urgently felt statements that I have bent to examine them at the level, so to speak, of their genetic code. That finely accommodated code gives them their urgency as worked art, without which their urgency as message would falter. To me, such poems offer the strongest contemporary testimony to the dependence of persuasive verbal art on a highly tempered sense of linguistic and formal implication going hand in hand with feeling and conviction.

Jorie Graham:
The Moment of Excess

◆ ◆ ◆

The breaking of style can occur on the largest scale, as when
Hopkins invents a new rhythm distinguishing his later poetry
from his earlier work; or it can occur, as in Heaney's writing, on
the scale of a single poem, as the adjectival style called for by the
poet's perplexity before the Grauballe Man is exchanged for the
nominal style demanded by the trance of a memory-portent in
"Deserted harbour stillness." Whereas a large-scale break in style
like Hopkins' can scarcely be ignored by readers and critics,
smaller breaks from poem to poem like Heaney's often go unno-
ticed, and the essential exposition through grammatical form of
the thematics of the poem goes unremarked. When a poem is
deprived, in critical discussion, of its material body—which is
constituted by its rhythm, its grammar, its lineation, or other such
features—it exists only as a mere cluster of ideas, and loses its
physical, and therefore its aesthetic, distinctness.

I want to look, in Jorie Graham's work, at the unit of the
individual line. Historically, the line has been the characteristic
unit distinguishing poetry from prose; it is the most sensitive
barometer of the breath-units in which poetry is voiced. The very
shortest way of composing a line makes a single word (in Cum-
mings and Berryman, even a single syllable or letter) constitute a
line; the very longest manner of composition invents a line that

spills over into turnovers, or, in a different move, suspends from its right margin an appended short line, what Hopkins called an "outride." When a poet ceases to write short lines and starts to write long lines, that change is a breaking of style almost more consequential, in its implications, than any other. Jorie Graham began as a writer of short poems in short lines, lines with a hesitant rhythm so seductive that one's heart, reproducing those poems, almost found a new way to beat. And then, with a burst of almost tidal energy, Graham began to publish long poems in long lines, poems that pressed toward an excess nearly uncontainable by the page. "Poetry," said Keats, "should surprise by a fine excess" (*Letters*, I, 238), and one form of that fine excess is the long line. "In excess, continual, there is cure for sorrow," Stevens observed in "A Weeping Burgher" (*Collected Poems*, 61), and one of those cures for world-sorrow is the independent, provocative, and exhilarating excess of voicing represented by the long line. Graham's breaking of style, from short lines to long, invites us to consider these and other possible implications of her act.

But before I come to Graham's recourse to the long line, it may be useful to say a word about the general presence of the lengthened line in modern verse. There are two chief classical sources of the long line—the epic hexameter and the dithyrambic lyric: the first stands for heroic endeavor, the second for ecstatic utterance. When Hopkins compared "The Wreck of the Deutschland" to a Pindaric ode, he wanted to reclaim ecstatic and irregular form beyond what the eighteenth century had done; but it was chiefly in his sonnets, as we have seen, that he pushed the regular English line to its utmost length, for both effortful and ecstatic reasons. Toward the end of his life, he wrote of his "herds-long" lines:

My cries heave, herds-long; huddle in a main, a chief-
Woe, wórld-sòrrow; on an áge-old ánvil wínce and síng—
Then lull, then leave off.

(*Poetical Works*, 182)

His several hexameter sonnets sometimes added outrides and even a coda; and finally, in the octameter lines of "Spelt from Sibyl's Leaves," Hopkins reached his breath-limit. As we have seen, Hopkins used the long line in several ways—as a container of heterogeneity, for instance, which could nonetheless rise to epic heroism: "Thís Jack, jóke, poor pótsherd, patch, | matchwood, immortal diamond / Is immortal diamond" (198). More interestingly, even, Hopkins used the long line to creep up on something by a chromatic series of words, each one melting ecstatically into the next by almost insensible half-steps: "Earnest, earthless, equal, attuneable, | vaulty, voluminous, . . . stupendous / Evening strains to be tíme's vást, | womb-of-all, home-of-all, hearse-of-all night" (190).

Like Hopkins, Whitman—who brought us the founding American free-verse line, deriving it from the Bible and Macpherson's *Ossian*—found the long line useful as a container for the heterogeneous; but he also used it to signify intellectual and speculative difficulties. It served Whitman, in its Hebraic coordinate form, for his ongoing repudiation of the old and embrace of the new: "I do not offer the old smooth prizes, but offer rough new prizes" (*Leaves of Grass*, 155). He also used it to signify spontaneity of speculation, and a ready turn to self-correction, as in the poem "Of the Terrible Doubt of Appearances," where a single line (l. 9) says of appearances:

> May-be [they are] seeming to me what they are (as doubtless
>   they indeed but seem) as from my present point of view,
>   and might prove (as of course they would) nought of what
>   they appear, or nought anyhow, from entirely changed
>   points of view.

> (120)

In spite of examples of length like those offered by Hopkins and Whitman, the English line tends stubbornly, when left to itself, to return to its more normative four- or five-beat length unless special heed is paid by the poet either toward shortening it—as Heaney deliberately did, for instance, in his volume *North* when he was seeking a more "Irish" music—or toward prolonging it, as Stevens did in a poem of Odyssean ongoingness called "Prologues to What Is Possible":

> He belonged to the far-foreign departure of his vessel and
>   was part of it,
> Part of the speculum of fire on its prow, its symbol, whatever
>   it was,
> Part of the glass-like sides on which it glided over the
>   salt-stained water,
> As he traveled alone, like a man lured on by a syllable
>   without any meaning.
>
> (*Collected Poems,* 516)

More could be said about the reasons why Whitman, Hopkins, and Stevens were pressed toward lengthening the English line— lengthening it against prescription, against historical habit, almost (one could say) against nature. But I want to move on to Graham, and ask why this pressure arises in her, so that her recent poems sprawl across the page in ways that startle and unsettle us, even while we are enthralled by their urgency, their effort, and their power.

The body Graham first chose for herself in verse was one that above all represented *deliberation.* That deliberation could be seen—to invoke an organic metaphor she uses in the recent poem "Opulence" (from *Materialism*)—as a stalk which arises slowly, puts forth a leaf, matches that leaf with another leaf on the opposite side of the stem, ascends a bit further, issues a branchlet, and then presses that branchlet to grow a twig. The narrow poems in Graham's first two books grew by antiphonal lines—the first line flush left, the second indented, the third flush left, the fourth indented, and so on. Step by step, accreting perceptions, the verse—to invoke a different metaphor—descended the page, cre-

ating a stairway (often of dimeter followed by monometer) for
the reader. Here is a fragment of "Scirocco" from her second
book, *Erosion* (1983):

> Outside his window
>   you can hear the scirocco
> working
>   the invisible.
> Every dry leaf of ivy
>   is fingered,
>
> refingered. Who is
>   the nervous spirit
> of this world
>   that must go over and over
> what it already knows,
>   what is it
>
> so hot and dry
>   that's looking through us,
> by us,
>   for its answer?
>
>   (8–9)

We see in such lines, which owe much to Williams, the young
poet's approach, increment by increment, to a mastery of the
world. Most of the poems in *Erosion,* a book written in Graham's
late twenties and early thirties, are composed in these stair-step
short lines. They embody a process the poet at times calls erosion,
at times dissection, in which something is crumbled, bit by bit,
to dust; or something is opened, layer by layer, to view.

The process of step-by-step investigation of the world is itself
defended in the central question, "How far is true?" posed by
Graham's harrowing poem "At Luca Signorelli's Resurrection of

the Body." The son of the painter Signorelli has died, and the
father, reaching beyond his grief, dissects the body:

> . . . He cut
> deeper,
> graduating slowly
> from the symbolic
>
> to the beautiful. How far
> is true?
> . . . . .
>
> . . . With beauty and care
> and technique
> and judgement, [he] cut into
> shadow, cut
> into bone and sinew and every
> pocket
>
> in which the cold light
> pooled.
> It took him days
> that deep
> caress, cutting,
> unfastening,
>
> until his mind
> could climb into
> the open flesh and
> mend itself.
>
> (76–77)

This accomplished, steady, unflinching writing-in-short-lines (which
deals out the lines, group by group, in regular six-line stanzas)

represents, we could say, a faith in the power of the patience of mind; and in its deliberate respect for the resistance of matter, it intimates the "beauty and care / and technique / and judgement" that the mind must observe in the precise investigative use of its various scalpels. The question "How far is true?" is left open-ended, but that it is the poet's duty to take the symbolic through the beautiful into the true is not in doubt.

Toward the end of *Erosion,* Graham includes a disturbing poem called "Updraft," its title betraying a force which is the diametrical opposite of those sequential, incremental, and orderly processes—whether natural like erosion or intellectual like dissection—on which Graham's form had depended. The updraft, or convection current, of Graham's poem literally turns the atmosphere turbulently upside-down in tumultuous irregular lines:

> . . . All the blossoms ripped suddenly by one gust, one
> updraft—mosaic
>
> of dust and silks
> by which we are all rising, turning, all
> free.

(70)

The movement chronicled by "Updraft" is the dissolution of meaning into unmeaning. The poet, now distrusting the closure of form, implores a God-like figure to let Eve, the mother of creation, symbol of the world of formed shapes, slip back into the uncreated:

> . . . so let her slip
>
> out of her heavy garment then, let her slip back
> into the rib, into Your dreams, Your
> loneliness, back, deep into the undress. . . .

(71)

The undress exists "back / before Your needle leapt in Your fingers, meaning." The "undress," then, that the poet longs for is what Kristeva calls by the Platonic name of the *chora*—the presymbolic matrix of language, where rhythm and syllable and semiosis have not yet coalesced into sign and meaning. But since we cannot go backward to the *chora*, we must, in our resistance to closure, go forward, by entropy, into randomness and shapelessness.

The long line, therefore, is first generated by Graham as the formal equivalent of mortality, dissolution, and unmeaning. At this point in her writing, it is set against the persuasions of shapely organic form, and against the intellectual intelligibility that is the result of careful deliberative investigation. "The blood," says Graham in "Updraft," "smears itself against the mind," and this contest, as suffering body disfigures questing spirit, is continued in all of Graham's later books.

Erosion was followed by the volume uncompromisingly entitled *The End of Beauty* (1987), which marks Graham's definitive break with short-lined lyric. Though the old investigative antiphonies reappear once or twice ("Eschatological Prayer," "Noli Me Tangere"), the preeminent move in the book is a struggle against the intellectual and formal dénouement of shapely closure. Rather, there is now in the poet an assent—voiced in a long-lined poem called "Vertigo"—to uncertainty and unpredictability: this is the vertigo felt as one abandons old and predetermined ways in favor of the pull of the unknown beyond the precipice of the new:

> She leaned out. What is it pulls at one, she wondered,
> What? That it has no shape but point of view?
> That it cannot move to hold us?
> Oh it has vibrancy, she thought, this emptiness, this intake
>   just
>   prior to
> the start of a story, the mind trying to fasten
> and fasten, the mind feeling it like a sickness this wanting

to snag, catch hold, begin, the mind crawling out to the edge
   of the cliff
and feeling the body as if for the first time—how it cannot
   follow, cannot love.

(The End of Beauty, 67)

The dizzying extension of the mind, as it crawls out to the edge
of the cliff of the conceptual, presses Graham to her long lines
and to their "outrides"—small piece-lines dropping down at the
right margin of their precursor-line. Graham's combination of
indefinitely stretching right-edge horizontality with occasional
right-edge vertical drops refuses both the model of step-by-step
upward mental advance and the model of investigative penetra-
tion inward from the beautiful into the true. Rather, Graham
redefines the human aim of verse as an earthly, terrain-oriented
lateral search (which can reach even the epic dimensions of the
Columbian voyage) rather than a vertical Signorelli-like descent
into depth or, as in "Updraft," ascent into prayer. Earthly desire
itself is the thing allegorized by Graham's long horizontal line,
desire always prolonging itself further and further over a gap it
nonetheless does not wish to close. In this search by desire, mind
will always outrun body. And the linear ongoingness necessitated
by the continuation of desire means that the absence of shape,
far from meaning dissolution and mortality, now stands for life
itself.

In the poem "Pollock and Canvas," Graham, searching for a
nontranscendent vertical which will be comparable to her earthly
"desiring" horizontal, finds a metaphor for her line in the fluid
drip of Pollock's paint between the body of the artist and his
canvas spread on the ground. The line of paint, let down from
the brush, is like a fishing line sinking without effort into the
water: this cascading line is not epic, like the Odyssean one
questingly covering distances toward a horizon; rather, it is ec-
static, living in the possible:

17

the line being fed out the line without shape before it lands
  without death

18

saying a good life is possible, still hissing still unposited,

19

before it lands, without shape, without generation, or form
  that bright fruit[.]

(84–85)

At this moment, the long vertical line, "fed out," is pure middle-
ness, the unposited, the possible, the "formless," the ethically
indeterminate. It has not yet tethered itself to shape, to ending,
to decision; it has not yet plucked the apple of the Fall.

To write a poetry of middleness, of suspension, is Graham's
chief intellectual and emotional preoccupation in *The End of Beauty*.
In that aim, she defers closure in many poems by a series of
ever-approaching asymptotic gestures, each one of them num-
bered, and each advancing the plot by a micro-measure. Her
model for this use of the long line seems to be the cinematic
freeze-frame, by which an action sequence in film is divided, like
the flight of Zeno's arrow, into minutely brief "shots," or ele-
ments. To place each of her elements into stop-time, Graham tries
the experiment of numbering the freeze-frames sequentially, so
that the unfamiliar appearance of a number punctuates on the
page each quantum of perception delivered by a line or lines.

This experiment—affixing a number to each perception-
packet—is tried in only six of the twenty-six poems in *The End of
Beauty*, but these six are the dual self-portraits in which the
volume finds its cohesion:

"Self-Portrait as the Gesture between Them"
"Self-Portrait as Both Parties"

"Self-Portrait as Apollo and Daphne"
"Self-Portrait as Hurry and Delay"
"Self-Portrait as Demeter and Persephone"
"Pollock and Canvas"

These poems have a collective importance beyond their mere number. Why, we must ask, does this forcibly stopped numbered version of the long line predominate in the self-portraits (of which "Pollock and Canvas," despite its title, is surely one)?

The self-portrait, as a visual genre, has always depended on some mirror-strategy by which the painter can depict an object normally inaccessible to vision: his or her own face. Not all self-portraits display the necessary mirror, but even those that do not do so prompt the viewer to some reflection on the difficulty of realization necessitated by such a portrait. Some self-portraits—Vermeer's of the artist in his studio, for instance—obliterate the face of the artist, as Vermeer substitutes the inscrutable rear view with black hat as an index of that necessary but suppressed subjectivity of the painter which plays a role in every painting, no matter how "objective." Parmigianino, as Ashbery has reminded us, paints himself reflected in a convex mirror so as to emphasize the distortion inevitable in any stratagem for self-representation.

Graham's facing up to the complex strategy of her own dual self-portraits is articulated most visibly in her numerically interrupted frames. They say: "Look at yourself in a frozen moment; write it down. Gaze again; write it down. And now glance a third time; and write it down." The alternations of consciousness as the pen succeeds the gaze are not concealed; rather, they are inscribed on the page, number by succeeding number. By "baring the device," as the Russian Formalists would say, Graham's self-portraits prevent an easy slide by the reader—or by the poet herself—into an introspection unconscious of problems of representation.

But what does the affixing of prefatory numbers have to do with Graham's break into the long line? The conventional view of the poetic line, as I have said, associates it with breath; and indeed, a good deal of theorizing about the material base of poetry links it to the inspiration and suspiration of the single breath as its measure. The physiological regulation of breathing makes natural breaths roughly isometric—in, out; in, out. And isometric breathing is the basis for regular lines, orderly and successive ones. But the gaze has no such isometric rhythm: a gaze can be prolonged at will, held for inspection, meditated on, and periodically interrupted. It is the gaze, rather than the breath, that seems to me Graham's fundamental measure in the numbered-line poems. By this choice of the gaze over the breath, Graham redefines utterance; and what utterance becomes is the tracking of the gaze, quantum-percept by quantum-percept, bundle by bundle. In Graham's recent poetry, a trust in the vagaries of the perceptual replaces the earlier poetry's trust both in the physiologically regulated order of breath and in a teleologically regulated order of truth. Since the apotheosis of the perceptual is necessarily an apotheosis of the moment, Graham is as interested in the (numbered) interruptive pause as in the significant perception; and her sequestering of the pause as a good in itself can be seen most clearly in "Pollock and Canvas," the most interesting test, in *The End of Beauty*, of her freeze-frame lines.

"Pollock and Canvas" is a poem in three Roman-numeraled parts, but only Part II affixes numbers to its lines. Part I is a conceptual summary (in the past tense) of Pollock's "drip" practice, linking him with the wounded King of *The Waste Land* and the Parsifal legends, a King suspended between life and death. The intermediate state of the King—alive but not life-giving, wounded but not dead—is summed up in Pollock's question as he bends over his canvas, refusing to let the brushtip touch it: *"tell me then what will render / the body alive?"* (*The End of Beauty*, 82). Pollock, though accomplished in the conferring of shape, resolves to keep his canvas safe from the death of final formal shape (*"his brush able to cut a figure / on the blank and refusing"*).

I pass over, for the moment, the numbered Part II, to look at
the way the poem concludes. Pollock's Part I terror of the con-
clusiveness of final shape is answered in Part III of "Pollock and
Canvas," which envisages a way *out* of formal shape. That formal
shape (beauty, love, the figure), once it has been conferred on the
canvas, permanently settles over a piece of life and determines it.
The only way out of the conclusiveness of that formal shape is
the admission into it of elements of chance; and Graham's figure
for that possibility is God's rest after He made the world, a point
at which the unintended, the serpent, can slip into Paradise:

> And then He rested, is that where the real
making
> begins—the now—Then He rested letting in chance
> letting in
any wind any shadow quick with minutes, and whimsy,
> through the light, letting the snake the turning
in.

(87)

Graham's conclusion is that the adventitious, the aleatory, the
not-yet-true will eventually, without God's intending it, become
part of the Creation:

> . . . Then things not yet true
> which slip in
are true,
> aren't they?

The things which slip in are part of the Keatsian "fine excess,"
and, since they are a "supplement" to what was intended, have
their formal equivalent in whatever in the line seems arbitrary,
unintended, added by chance, as though the line had had to
expand to take such things in.

In "Pollock and Canvas," long lines exist, it is true, in both the Amfortas-suspension of Part I and the Jehovah-chance of Part III. But the quintessence of the species "long line" in the volume *The End of Beauty*—which I take to be the long line intermitted by the long numbered pause—is achieved in Part II of "Pollock and Canvas," where, though Pollock cannot entirely avoid the forward pull of temporality, he attempts to spatialize time as much as possible by inserting between each gaze a pause, representing ecstatic being:

Part II

1

Here is the lake, the open, he calls it his day; fishing.

2

The lake, the middle movement, women's flesh, maya.

3

And here is the hook before it has landed, before it's deep in
the current[.]

(82–83)

This pregnant section of the poem—enacting space, middleness, incarnation, illusion, suspension—speaks directly of what the double excess of the long line and the long pause mean to Graham—a way of representing the luxurious spread of experienced being, preanalytic and precontingent. This condition has Romantic affinities; but Graham does not want to be laid asleep in body to become a living soul. Rather, against Wordsworth, she almost wants to be laid asleep in mind to become a living body. Her *maya* contains no access to Wordsworthian transcendence; rather, she accepts its blessed stoppage in prolonged sensual illusion, that excess that is, in Stevens' terms, the cure of sorrow. The incarnation of this *maya* as it takes place "between the creator and the created" (83) is the Stevensian moment of credences of summer, of human existence without temporal entrance or exit, represented paradoxically by "of the graces the / 8 / most violent one, the one all gash, all description." This grace is the Muse of eternal process, who has replaced for Graham the meditated, investigative, and shaped Muse of product.

Graham's long line, representing being-in-process, continues, after *The End of Beauty,* into *Region of Unlikeness* (1991); but in the later, more autobiographical volume, the line drops its earlier partner, the open numbered space, which had represented being-in-pause. The gaze turns to single autobiographical self-portrait (which replaces mythological dual self-portrait), and the plot of narrative replaces bundled quanta of perception. Instead of dwelling on *Region of Unlikeness,* I want to turn to Graham's most recent book, *Materialism* (1993), because in it she combines the long line with its apparently ultimate narrative partner, the long sentence. Since the long horizontal line of extension in space toward the horizon is itself already formally effortful, it becomes even more epically taxing when it is joined to the long sentence (the conventional equivalent of temporal and conceptual complexity). To the long horizontal axis is added a long vertical axis. Graham had used long sentences to good effect as early as *Erosion,* but there they were strung down the page in very short lines. In *The End of Beauty,* the lines were longer, but the long sentences appearing there were usually interspersed with shorter ones, alleviating the effort of suspension. In *Materialism,* the combination of horizontal and vertical prolongation is carried out to the utmost degree, so that the poems literally construct visual plane areas ("tarpaulins," to use Ashbery's word from the poem of that name) in which words cover and spatialize being.

Total coverage is the ultimate effect toward which Graham has been tending with her long lines ever since they first appeared. This area-effect has affinities with other literary structures (the

epic simile, the Miltonic verse-paragraph, the Whitmanian cata-
logue, the Moore encyclopedia-page), since all of these represent
what Graham calls, in one of the titles of *Materialism,* "The
Dream of the Unified Field." In that dream (in Graham's ver-
sion), the whole world is extrapolated out from whatever center
one chooses as origin. Stevens conceived of this effect, in "The
Man with the Blue Guitar," as one in which the twang of the blue
guitar would be "the reason in the storm," incorporating the
whole of the storm while giving it a focal point and intelligibility:

> I know my lazy, leaden twang
> Is like the reason in a storm;
>
> And yet it brings the storm to bear.
> I twang it out and leave it there.
> (*Collected Poems,* 169)

Against Stevens' brisk storm, we can put Graham's enveloping
storm in *Materialism:*

> The storm: I close my eyes and,
> standing in it, try to make it *mine.*
> . . . possession
> gripping down to form,
> wilderness brought deep into my clearing,
> out of the ooze of night,
> limbed, shouldered, necked, visaged, the white—
> now the clouds coming in (don't look up),
> now the Age behind the clouds, The Great Heights,
> all in there, reclining, eyes closed, huge,
> centuries and centuries long and wide,
> and underneath, barely attached but attached,

like a runner, my body, my tiny piece of
the century—minutes, houses going by—The Great
                                        Heights—
anchored by these footsteps, now and now,
the footstepping—now and now—carrying its vast
white sleeping geography—mapped—
not a lease—*possession*.

(*Materialism*, 85–86)

Graham compares this constant human desire for aesthetic pos-
session of all space and time (the Great Heights, the long and
wide centuries) to Columbus' desire to possess the New World;
the hubristic dubiety of both enterprises is set against their spiri-
tual ambition. Such undertakings are instinctive and unavoidable,
Graham suggests, in creatures of mind and appetite. The human
appetite desires metaphysical and intellectual, as much as material,
gain. It is the limitlessness of the claims of intellect and of desire
that Graham's recent ambitious poems are most inspired by, and
most appalled by as well.

The appetitiveness of the mind, and the infinity of the world's
stimuli, generate the excess of Graham's long horizontal lines,
which generate, in their turn, her long vertical sentences. Any
given poetic idea begins to produce, in Graham, a version of an
aesthetic Big Bang with its vertiginous perceptual expansion and
its receding conceptual distances. We can see this happening in
the recent unpublished poem "The Turning." The poem is about
dawn in an Italian hill town, and it begins with several brief
successive noticings (not quoted here). Each noticing creates a
brief sentence, and then stops. Nothing can take wing. The poet
cannot yet feel her way into the heterogeneity, simultaneity, chro-
matic change, spontaneity, and self-correction present in all acts
of extended noticing. Eventually, the reason for the fizzling-out
of each perception is formulated: there is either a war between

the world and its perceiver, preventing their interpenetration; or else there is an indifference between them, making them remain on parallel tracks without intersection:

> There is a war.
> Two parallels that will not meet have formed
> a wall.

In spite of successive tries, the desired tarpaulin, area, square, updraft, thrown cloth, has not yet been found. Not until inner feeling and outer perception begin to meld, and the poet's body becomes, kinesthetically, a form of the world's fluid body, can the world be re-created in language. The poet declares her creed: that the sun must come up in her before it can come up on her page; and it must come up on her page before it can come up for her reader:

> The sun revolves because of our revolving in
>   the wall.

The wall is the poet's new perceptual blank sheet of paper. At the beginning of her observation of the dawn, nothing is inscribed on her mental "wall" except Stevens' command to himself at the end of "Notes toward a Supreme Fiction," where he addresses the Earth, saying that poetry requires *"that I / should name you"*:

> Fat girl, terrestrial, my summer, my night,
> How is it I find you in difference, see you there
> In a moving contour, a change not quite completed?
>
>   . . . This unprovoked sensation requires
>
> That I should name you flatly, waste no words,
> Check your evasions, hold you to yourself.

             . . . You
Become the soft-footed phantom, the irrational

Distortion.
                                    (*Collected Poems,* 406)

Faced with her recollection of Stevens' command, Graham, "phantom-eyed," must name the "soft-footed phantom," the earth as it presents itself on this Italian morning. But how is she to articulate the area, the cloth, the tarpaulin to be cast over this infinitely opening piece of reality without stiffening it into life-lessness?

It is within the moment of an unlooked-for chance event, when a single bird moves, that the poet finds she can rise unexpectedly with it into unimpeded voice, combining bird, soul, light, church-bells, swallow-flocks, and human beings into a single long—almost unending—sentence which constructs the second part of the poem (quoted here) from the words "Bright whites and citrines" to "I look down into the neighbor's garden":

             . . . Bright whites and citrines
                   gleaming forth,
   layerings, syllables of
             the most loud
             invisible
   that stick (no departure and no return) to their single
                                        constantly revised
   (I saw men yesterday, tuck-pointing, on their scaffold)
   lecture on what
   most matters: sun: now churchbells breaking up
                             in twos and threes
                             the flock
   which works across in
                   granular,

forked, suddenly cacophonic
      undulation
      (though at the level
of the inaudible) large differences of rustling, risings and
   lowerings,
                               swallowings of
                               silence where the wings
en masse lift off—and then the other (indecipherable) new
                        silence where
                        wings aren't
used and the flock floats in
unison—
        a flying-in-formation sound which
I can see across the wall (as if loud)—shrapnel of
                    blacknesses
                    against the brightnesses—
fistfuls thrown (as if splattered) then growing fantastically
                        in size (also now
                        rising swiftly) as
they come—a stem of silence which blossoms suddenly
as it vanishes from the wall—(turning, the whole
                            flock
turning) exfoliation of aural clottings where all wings open
   now
                               to break
and pump—vapor of accreting inaudibles—
innermost sound scratchy with clawed and necked
                        and winged
indecipherables (a herald)—whole flock now rising highest
   just before it
turns to write the longest version yet against the whole
length of the wall where the churchbells
have begun to cease and

one name is called out (but low, down near the Roman
                                    gate) and one
car from down there sputters
up—(the light brightest now, it almost
true morning)—
these walls these streets the light the shadow in them
the throat of the thing—birds reassembling over the roof
in syncopated undulations of cooing as they settle . . .
I look down into the neighbor's garden.

In order to maintain itself, this long-lined and outridered long
sentence depends on several grammatical techniques of prolon-
gation—present participles, appositions, relative clauses both ad-
jectival and adverbial, parenthetical insertions, a colon, additive
conjunctions like "and," negations, comparisons ("as if"), co-
temporalities ("also"), successivities ("then" and "just before"),
repetitions ("now . . . now"), qualifications, and nominal simul-
taneities ("these walls these streets the light the shadow in them
/ the throat of the thing").

It is only of course after the fact that we can name these
grammatical means accelerating the perceptual thrust of the sen-
tence; during our actual stretched assimilation of this long cascade
of words flung over a page we are, to put it imaginatively, partici-
pating in making the sun come up, the birds awaken, and the
churchbells ring. Such an epic sentence—as the town turns from
night to morning—is a human, and therefore effortful, *Fiat lux*.
It cannot have the concision and effortlessness of the divine
illumination of chaos, because it is made from a human sensing
and concentrating body striving to comprehend a moment in one
internalized physical and mental gestalt. And that human body is
replicating *itself* in its aesthetic body of words, rather than repli-
cating the outside world in a direct mimesis. The poet has to
substitute, for the metaphysical divine will and the intellectual

divine Logos, a frail human eye and an even frailer human will, which must concentrate fiercely to translate into internal kines- thetic sense-response "the most loud invisible" of the light and "the vapor of accreting inaudibles," the silent flocking of birds. The poet must translate these first into a consciousness of her own internal physical mimicry of the external stimuli, and then, in turn, she must translate that internal kinesthetic mimicry into the visible and audible signs of English, a language with its own internal constraints on expression. The order of linguistic sig- nification, which succeeds the orders of perception and kinesthe- sia, is represented in the poem by the moment when "one name is called out." Every genuine poem, as Mallarmé insisted, aims at being "one name"—a single complex and indivisible unit of lan- guage proper to its moment and irreplaceable by any other. As the poet lifts the silent and the nonlinguistic and the nonpropo- sitional from perceptual import to kinesthetic import into semi- otic and rhythmic import, one form of suffering—seeing the day go by unregistered and unrecorded—is brought to an end.

The poet's subsidence into rest—after the epic but also ecstatic effort of turning dawn into words—is almost painfully brief: "I look down into the neighbor's garden." There are still things unheard, the poet reminds herself (the petal-fall); there are still things her transcription has been unable to incorporate (the pine tree unincluded in the long central sentence):

> What if I could hear the sound of petals falling
> off the head that
> holds them
> when it's time?
> What if I could hear where something is suddenly
> complete?
> The pinetree marionette-like against the wall—but still,
> unused.
> Whose turn is it now? Whose?

A new sentence begins to brew in the poet's compelled heart: she has "done" one bit of morning, the turn from dark to light, from nested birds to flying flocks, from silence to churchbells, from sleep to the crying of a single name—but "Whose turn is it now? Whose?"

The alternating rhythms of silence and naming become ever more anguishing in Graham's work, if only because each poem, at this point in her pursuit of the lyric, demands of her that she leave out nothing. This is a demand to which all serious artists eventually come—"O mother, what have I left out? O mother, what have I forgotten?" asks Ginsberg in "Kaddish"—and, implicitly, all readers test long lyrics by asking "What *should* have been included here by way of observation, reflection, qualification, and conclusion, and was, to the detriment of the poem, left out?" (Even shorter lyrics must, to succeed, convince us of their completeness; they do it by a sort of Dickinsonian implosion, in which an implied prehistory of ignited totalization is condensed into charred post-hoc indices of itself.)

At this moment in her writing, Graham chooses to show us her expanding universe by means of a slice of it in conic section. The cosmological excess that Graham has been insisting on recently can be read as a corrective to the current lyric of personal circumscription. It is especially a corrective (in its descent from Dickinson at her most metaphysical and Moore at her most expansive) to the lack of grandeur in much contemporary American poetry. Just as the personal is always in danger of becoming petty, so of course the grand is always in danger of the grandiose; and the Great Heights (as Graham has called them) can, unchecked, become parodies of themselves. Graham's capacity to descend from the Great Heights to an unremarkable single dawn in an anonymous town suggests that she understands the Whitmanian ecstatic sublimity of the ordinary as well as the Shelleyan heroic sublimity of aspiration. She has shown, in still other poems, that she possesses self-irony and historical irony, both of them useful balances to the vaulting mind and the universalizing voice that have impelled her approach to the edge of the precipice of perception by means of her triple excess—her long lines, her long pauses, and her long sentences.

I said, when I began to consider the breaking of style, that it reflected a change of aesthetic body. Whether at the large level at which Hopkins turned to sprung rhythm to reflect his sense of the instress of the pied aesthetic moment; or at the mid-level at which Heaney distinguishes the gestalt of different poems by different parts of speech; or at the micro-level of the line, the pause, and the sentence, where Graham registers the movement from segmental investigative teleological patience to the ecstatic and heroic excess of totalizing phenomenological and kinesthetic perception, the breaking of style repays investigation. While it is true that we are initially *drawn* to poems by their passions, their questions, and their tonal urgencies, we are *convinced* by them, finally, insofar as they can invent formal means for their impelling motives. It is because I am struck, always, by a naive wonder at the convincingness of a poem that I feel driven to ask how that memorable persuasive power has been gained. "The only marvelous bishops of heaven," said Stevens in the essay "Two or Three Ideas," "have always been those that made it seem like heaven" (*Opus Posthumous*, 261). Hopkins—by making the aesthetic moment "seem so" in his shocks and stresses; Heaney—by making the Grauballe Man "seem so" in his combination of adjectival atrocity and beauty; Graham—by making the dawn "seem so" in her lifting "excessive," plane sentence-area of "excessive" lines— have put style, and the breaking of style, to enlightening use. The world never seems the same again when we go back to it after such poems. The style of our own inner kinesthetic motions has, through them, been broken and remade; and as Yeats reminds us, in moments of the breaking of style it is ourselves that we remake.

Works Cited

◆ ◆ ◆

Ashbery, John. *Reported Sightings*. New York: Knopf, 1988.

Corcoran, Neil. *Seamus Heaney*. London: Faber and Faber, 1986.

Graham, Jorie. *Erosion*. Princeton: Princeton University Press, 1983.

———— *The End of Beauty*. New York: Ecco Press, 1987.

———— *Materialism*. New York: Ecco Press, 1994.

Heaney, Seamus. *Selected Poems*. New York: Farrar, Straus, Giroux, 1990.

———— *Field Work*. New York: Farrar, Straus, Giroux, 1979.

———— *Preoccupations*. New York: Farrar, Straus, Giroux, 1980.

———— *Seeing Things*. New York: Farrar, Straus, Giroux, 1991.

Hopkins, Gerard Manley. *Poetical Works*. Ed. Norman H. Mackenzie. Oxford: Clarendon Press, 1990.

———— *Letters to Robert Bridges*. Ed. Claude Colleer Abbott. London: Oxford University Press, 1955.

———— *Correspondence of Gerard Manley Hopkins and Richard Watson Dixon*. Ed. Claude Colleer Abbott. London: Oxford University Press, 1955.

Keats, John. *Letters*. Ed. Hyder Rollins. 2 vols. Cambridge, Mass.: Harvard University Press, 1958.

Stevens, Wallace. *Collected Poems*. New York: Knopf, 1955.

———— *Letters*. New York: Knopf, 1966.

———— *Opus Posthumous*. New edition, ed. Milton Bates. New York: Knopf, 1989.

Whitman, Walt. *Leaves of Grass: Comprehensive Reader's Edition*. Ed. Harold W. Blodgett and Sculley Bradley. New York: New York University Press, 1965.

Yeats, W. B. *Collected Poems*. New York: Macmillan, 1956.

Index

• • •